268.63
WAT

D0422374

The Church of Christ
Tuscumbia, Alabama

TALK WITH YOUR HANDS

TALK WITH

YOUR **HANDS**

VOL. **2**

WRITTEN AND ILLUSTRATED BY

David O. Watson

No part of this book may be reproduced
by any mechanical, photographic, or electronic process,
nor may it be stored in a retrieval system, transmitted,
or otherwise copied for public or private use
without written permission of the publisher.

The original edition now in its 14th printing is still available.

First Printing January 1964

Reprintings:
April 1965
August 1966
May 1967
February 1968
October 1968
April 1969
November 1969
September 1970
January 1971
September 1971
January 1972
September 1972
March 1973

Available from the author and publisher
Route One
Winneconne, Wisconsin 54986

Copyright © 1973
David O. Watson, Jr.

Printed and Bound by
GEORGE BANTA COMPANY, INC.
Menasha, Wisconsin

PRINTED IN THE UNITED STATES OF AMERICA

This book is dedicated to the
two greatest people in my
life . . .

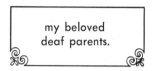

my beloved
deaf parents.

Acknowledgment . . .

It was my privilege and pleasure to accept an invitation to participate in the Midwest Manual Language Seminar at the Untermyer house, Deerfield, Illinois, in sessions for over nine months commencing June, 1970.

The seminar held no preconceived formula for the expansion and refinement of the manual language, but agreed that new sign evolve from intrinsic body-mind expressions with heavy reliance on existing signs.

New sign designed for small deaf children emerged through relentless co-operative efforts of a real cross-section of people who may have invested in the development of the manual language of the deaf people.

Ethel Untermyer, *mother of a six year old deaf child.*
Samuel A. Block, Bob Donoghue, Frank Sullivan, Leonard and Celia Warshawsky, *post lingually deafened individuals.*
Jerry Strom and Herbert Vollmar, *deaf.*
Kay Munro, *hearing daughter of deaf parents, M.A. Gallaudet, and D.V.R. Counselor.*
Candy Haight Smith, *hearing daughter of deaf parents and para-professional at Michael Reese Hospital.*
The Rev. Chester Nichols, *hearing pastor to the deaf.*
The Rev. and Mrs. Silas Hirte, *deaf Episcopal priest.*
Karen True, *teacher of deaf children.*
David Johnston, *hearing entymologist.*

The author would also like to express his appreciation to other individuals for their assistance and encouragement:

Dr. Byron B. Burnes, Marjorie Clere, the Milwaukee Journal, Bill Broomall, Rev. Duane King, Lucille Olson, and many others.

Foreword

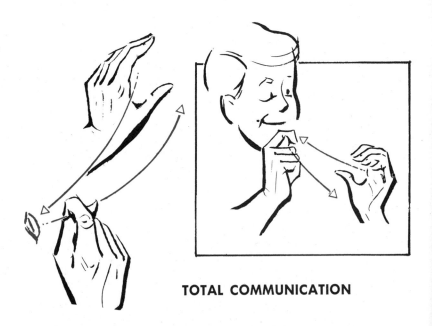

TOTAL COMMUNICATION

By Total Communication is meant the right of a deaf child to learn to use all forms of communication available to develop language competence at the earliest possible age. This implies introduction to a reliable receptive-expressive symbol system in the preschool years between the ages of one and five. Total Communication includes the full spectrum of language modes: child devised gestures, formal sign language, speech, speechreading, fingerspelling, reading and writing. Every deaf child must have the opportunity to develop any remanent of residual hearing for the enhancement of speech and speechreading skills through the use of individual and/or high fidelity group amplification systems.

Dr. David M. Denton, Supt.
Maryland School for the Deaf

Introduction

"*Talk With Your Hands*" has inevitably expanded itself into a virtual dictionary of the American Sign Language, or Ameslan,* for short. The original book conceived in 1960 and published in 1964 has gone into 14 reprintings, an acceptance for which the author is profoundly grateful. Because of such factors as the tremendous growth in sign language classes and the growing interest of persons of the hearing world and the following additional tabulations, a major revision comprising two volumes is in order: Through such revision, "*Talk With Your Hands*" can provide more than a greatly updated dictionary of the language of signs; it can serve as a textbook, as a reference work and as a reading source offering sheer enjoyment. Additionally, it can:

1) provide many new signs to fill an important need for small deaf children.
2) present an accurate visualization of hands in positions of correct perspectives.
3) assist the deaf and hearing-impaired persons in remote and isolated areas to keep informed about uniformity of standardized signs.
4) stimulate practice of deaf idioms as used in Ameslan.

Sign vocabulary is receiving increased attention. "What is the sign for . . .?" Also, "Have you heard the new sign for . . . ?" These are questions increasingly asked among teachers, students, parents of deaf and hearing-impaired children and also the various professional people within the educational framework. In recent years, there have been some very interesting innovations recorded in vocabulary. Example: The verb "to be" and its tenses. Also, new signs have been created or invented for words that previously had none— and thus had to be fingerspelled. Professionals in communications also remark on seeing refinements of signs that provide synonyms by use of initialization. There is also a need for practice sentences and phrases covering both the Signed English and the idiomatic expressions useful in various situations. All of these innovations and needs form part of the two volumes now offered.

Keeping abreast of such changes has required extensive travel and diligent association with the deaf, the teachers and the parents as they have met in seminars and various group meetings. As a result, the author has created and assembled over 3,000 formal signs. These include about 500 new signs invented and developed by various communication systems and by the artist.

The verb forms and tenses on pages 33-44 are designed for Signed English usage as part of the total communications program now used in many schools (the number of which is growing).

Students should first practice fingerspelling all small words and should "read" receiving fingerspelled words. This needs constant practice. Repetition is the best teacher. When introducing a new sign for the first time, it is advisable to make the sign, then fingerspell in case the receiver is not familiar with the sign. Idiomatic expression (deaf idioms) should be taught preferably by a skilled deaf or hearing Instructor at the same time the basic sign is learned.

* Ameslan is an acronym for American Sign Language as defined by Mr. Louie Fant, Jr. D.W.

VOLUME ONE . . . . . CONTENTS

VOLUME ONE . . . . . CONTENTS
(continued)

VOLUME TWO . . . . . CONTENTS

HOW TO READ, UNDERSTAND, AND REPEAT THE "ARRESTED" MOTION IN PRINT

Compare the two illustrations below. The little finger dipping in the closed hand represents a brush or pen in an inkwell. Next, as seen here by the red line and solid red arrow, the hand is brought up to the "sketch pad". This is followed with a few strokes with the little finger on the "pad" as indicated by the open-faced arrow.

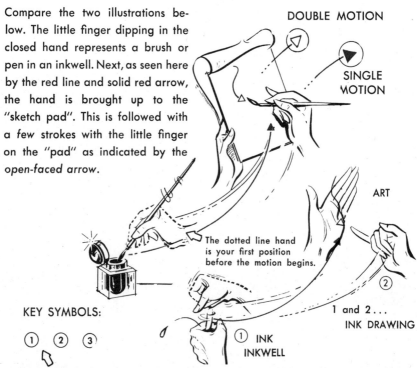

DOUBLE MOTION

SINGLE MOTION

ART

The dotted line hand is your first position before the motion begins.

1 and 2 ... INK DRAWING

KEY SYMBOLS:

① ② ③

① INK INKWELL

The circled numbers mean the combined signs are made in that order; and combining the two signs expresses the word or idea, "ink drawing". Sometimes a combination of three signs is formed to express an idea.

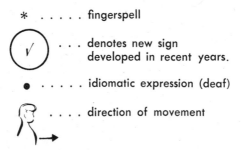

* . . . . . fingerspell

Ⓥ . . . denotes new sign developed in recent years.

● . . . . . idiomatic expression (deaf)

. . . . direction of movement

If you can't remember the sign . . . fingerspell!

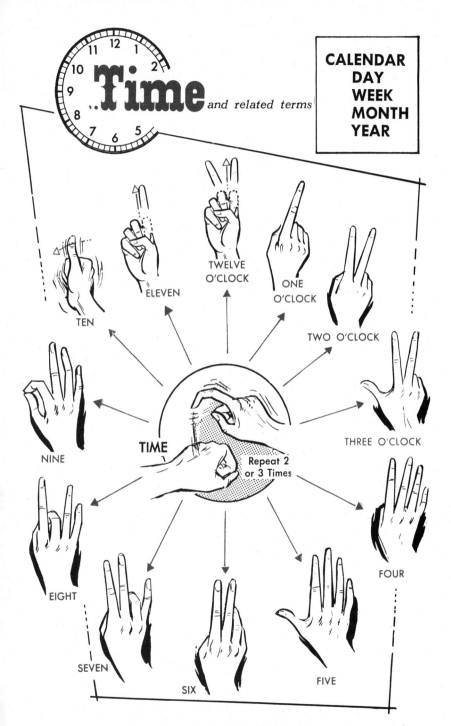

Time *and related terms*

CALENDAR
DAY
WEEK
MONTH
YEAR

TEN

ELEVEN

TWELVE O'CLOCK

ONE O'CLOCK

TWO O'CLOCK

THREE O'CLOCK

NINE

TIME

Repeat 2 or 3 Times

FOUR

EIGHT

SEVEN

SIX

FIVE

• "What time is it?"

"It's only 20 till 6. We have plenty of time"

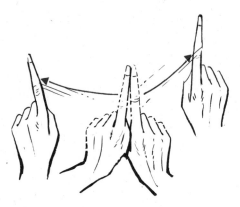

"We shall <u>part</u> and meet again at this corner"

FUTURE

290

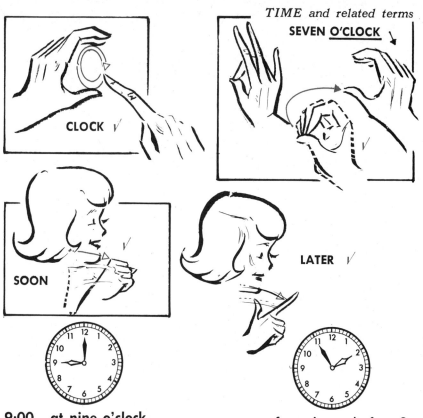

CLOCK √

SEVEN O'CLOCK

SOON

LATER √

9:00..at nine o'clock
(in the morning or at night?)

..a few minutes before 2
..just "shy" of two o'clock
..about two o'clock

7:30..at seven thirty

..a few minutes past 12
..three minutes after 12

4:00..at four o'clock

10:15..at ten fifteen
(fifteen after ten)

291

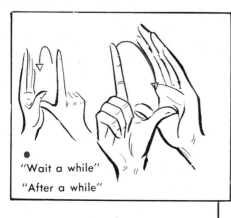

"Wait a while"

"After a while"

● "At the time"

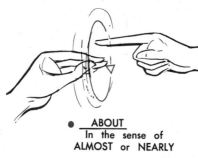

● ABOUT
In the sense of
ALMOST or NEARLY

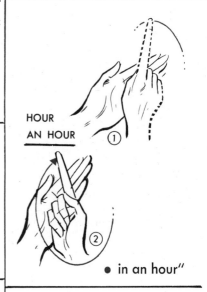

HOUR
AN HOUR ①

②

● in an hour"

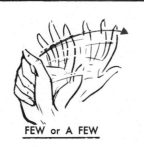

FEW or A FEW

● "..in a few moments"
few seconds"
"..in a jiffy"

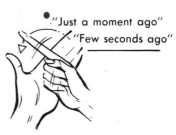

● "Just a moment ago"
"Few seconds ago"

292

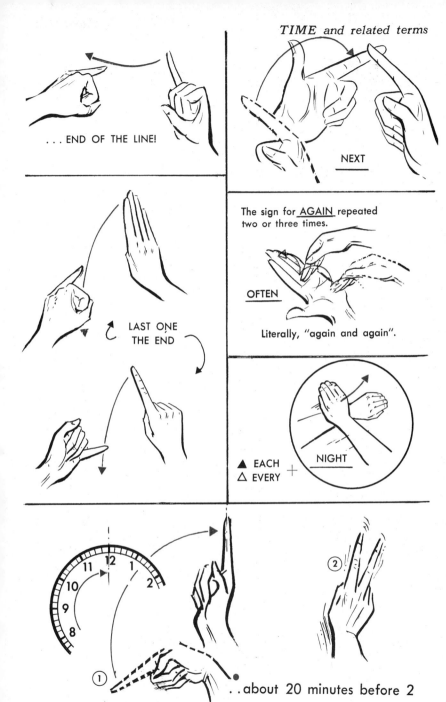

. . . END OF THE LINE!

TIME and related terms

NEXT

The sign for <u>AGAIN</u> repeated two or three times.

OFTEN

Literally, "again and again".

LAST ONE
THE END

▲ EACH
△ EVERY +

NIGHT

. .about 20 minutes before 2

293

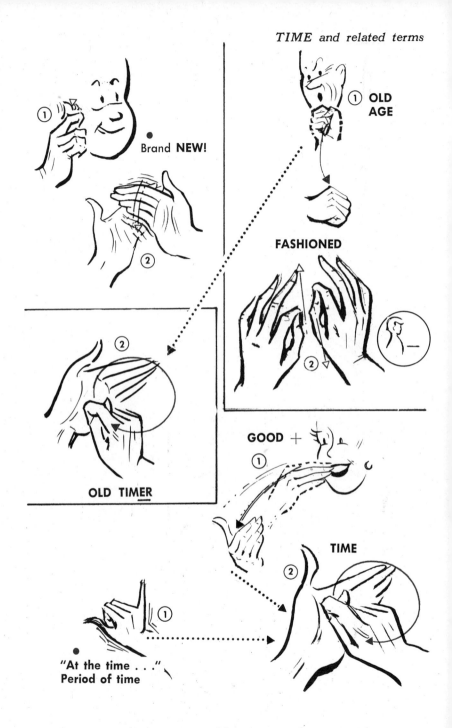

OLD
AGE

Brand **NEW!**

FASHIONED

OLD TIM**ER**

GOOD +

TIME

"At the time . . ."
Period of time

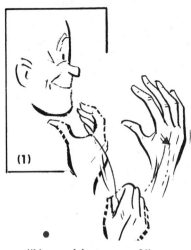

(1)

(2)

"GUESS?"

• "How old are you?"

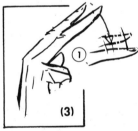

(3)

• "You appear to be about 39"

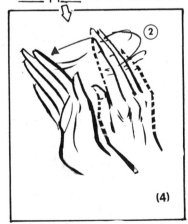

(4)

(5)

really

(6)

live

CHEST

(7)

up

(8)

"I am really going to
live it up, and have
a good time!"

good

(9)

(10)

(11)

"TRAVEL THROUGH . ."

(12)

(13)

also used for
• gallavanting

(14)

carnival

(15)

CIRCUS

YiPPiE!

(16)

297

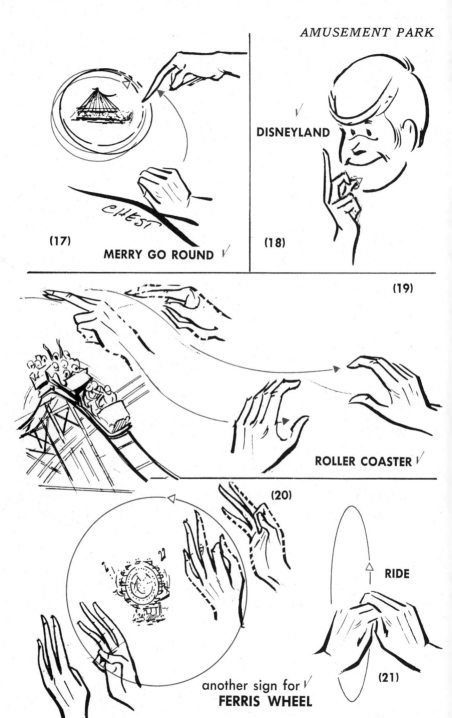

DISNEYLAND

(17)
MERRY GO ROUND √

(18)

(19)

ROLLER COASTER √

(20)

RIDE

another sign for √
FERRIS WHEEL

(21)

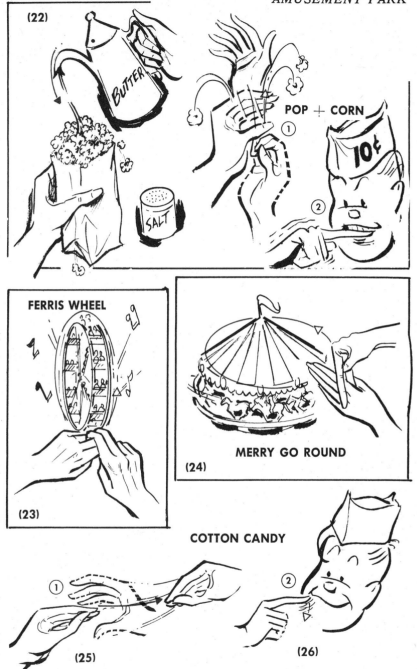

(22)

BUTTER

SALT

POP + CORN

10¢

FERRIS WHEEL

(23)

MERRY GO ROUND

(24)

COTTON CANDY

(25)

(26)

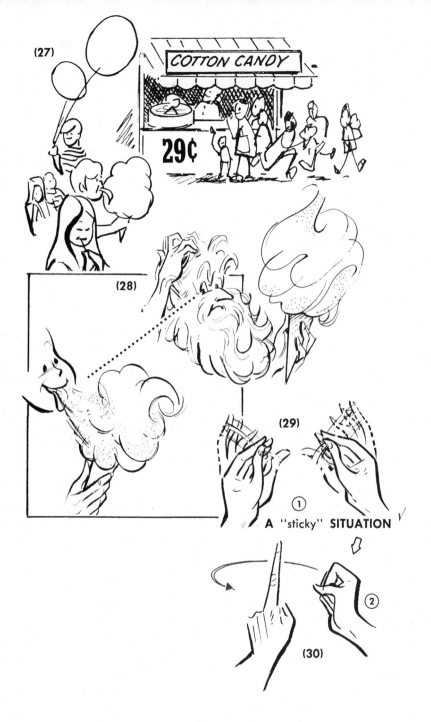

(27)

COTTON CANDY

29¢

(28)

(29)

① A "sticky" SITUATION

②

(30)

300

TIME *and related terms*

● "..up till now"
"..all along since"

"as usual"
(as + since)
"so far"

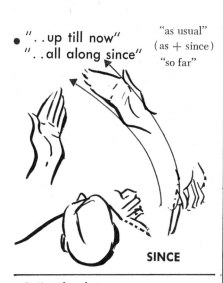

SINCE

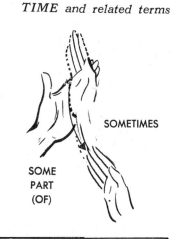

SOMETIMES

SOME
PART
(OF)

● ".. back in

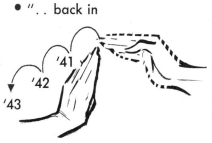

'41
'42
'43

OCCASIONALLY ●

"every so often"
"now and then"
"from time to time"
"once in a while"
"at times"

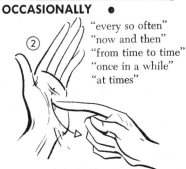

Repeat several times. The sign made slowly or rapidly indicates whether it is frequent or seldom.

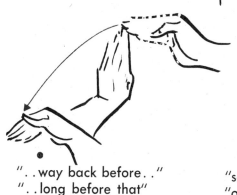

"..way back before.."
"..long before that"

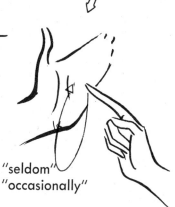

"seldom"
"occasionally"

301

● "... later on"
"... in the future"

or the letter **"F"**
for **FUTURE**

● "... far in the future"

● "year round"

"What did you do
last **WEEKEND?"**

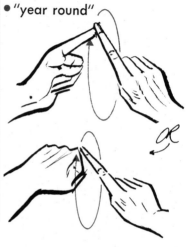

"... from January

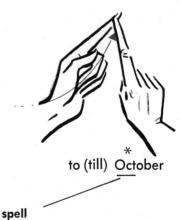

to (till) October

spell

302

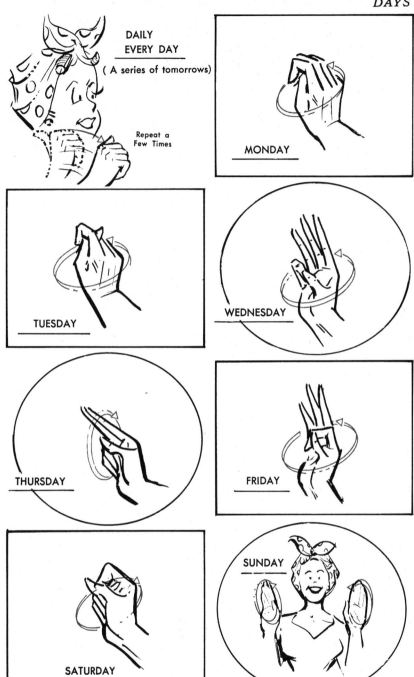

DAILY
EVERY DAY

(A series of tomorrows)

Repeat a
Few Times

MONDAY

TUESDAY

WEDNESDAY

THURSDAY

FRIDAY

SATURDAY

SUNDAY

303

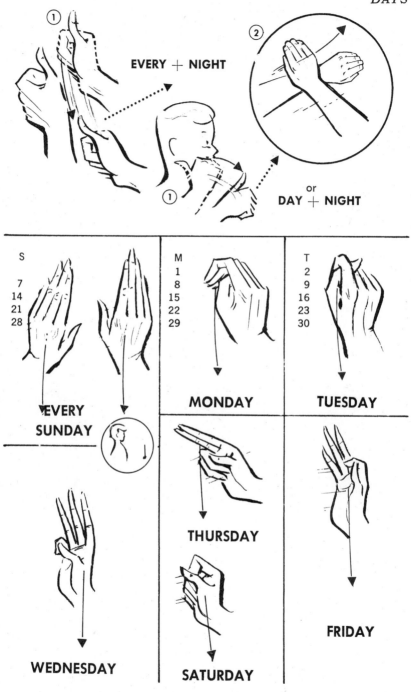

① EVERY + NIGHT

②

or
DAY + NIGHT

S
7
14
21
28

EVERY SUNDAY

M
1
8
15
22
29

MONDAY

T
2
9
16
23
30

TUESDAY

WEDNESDAY

THURSDAY

SATURDAY

FRIDAY

304

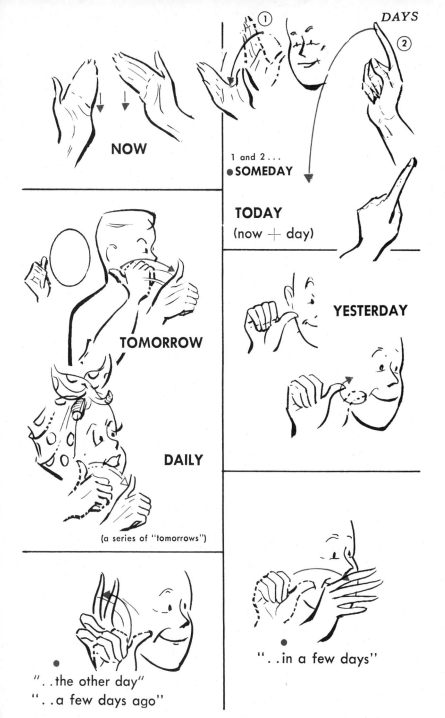

NOW

1 and 2...
● **SOMEDAY**

TODAY
(now + day)

DAYS

TOMORROW

YESTERDAY

DAILY

(a series of "tomorrows")

"..in a few days"

●
"..the other day"
"..a few days ago"

305

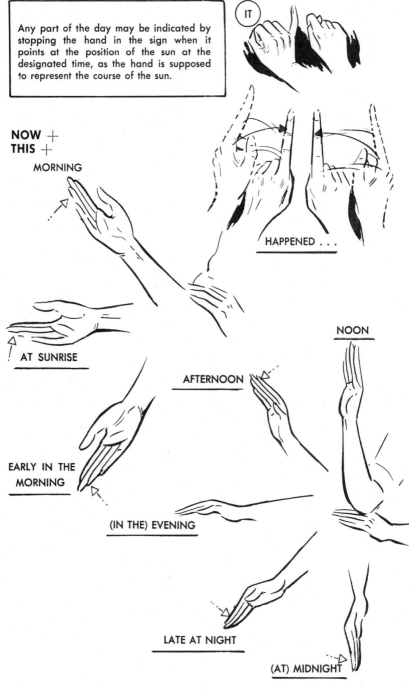

Any part of the day may be indicated by stopping the hand in the sign when it points at the position of the sun at the designated time, as the hand is supposed to represent the course of the sun.

IT

NOW +
THIS +
MORNING

HAPPENED . . .

AT SUNRISE

NOON

AFTERNOON

EARLY IN THE
MORNING

(IN THE) EVENING

LATE AT NIGHT

(AT) MIDNIGHT

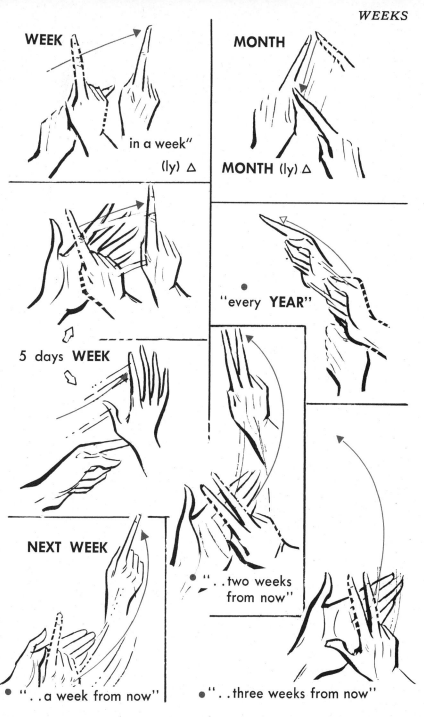

WEEK

in a week"

(ly) △

MONTH

MONTH (ly) △

5 days **WEEK**

"every **YEAR**"

NEXT WEEK

● ". . two weeks
from now"

● ". . . a week from now"

● ". . . three weeks from now"

307

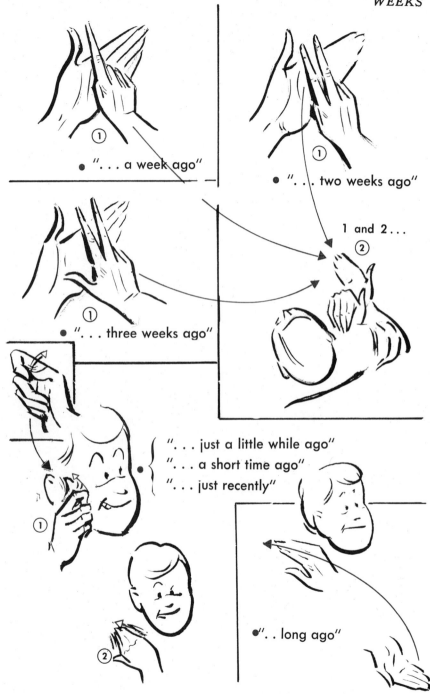

● "... a week ago"

● "... two weeks ago"

1 and 2...

● "... three weeks ago"

"... just a little while ago"
"... a short time ago"
"... just recently"

●"... long ago"

308

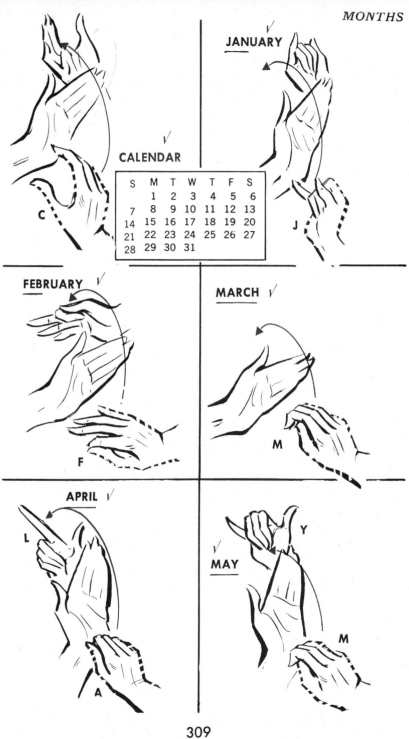

JANUARY

CALENDAR

S	M	T	W	T	F	S
	1	2	3	4	5	6
7	8	9	10	11	12	13
14	15	16	17	18	19	20
21	22	23	24	25	26	27
28	29	30	31			

C

J

FEBRUARY

MARCH

F

M

APRIL

L

MAY

A

Y

M

309

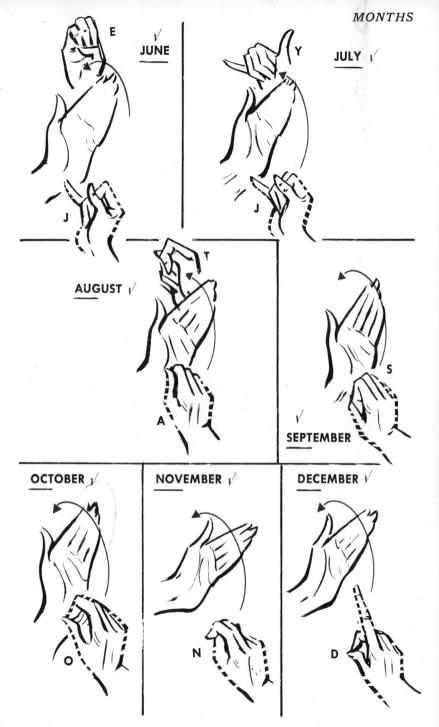

JUNE √

JULY √

AUGUST √

SEPTEMBER √

OCTOBER √

NOVEMBER √

DECEMBER √

310

HOLIDAYS

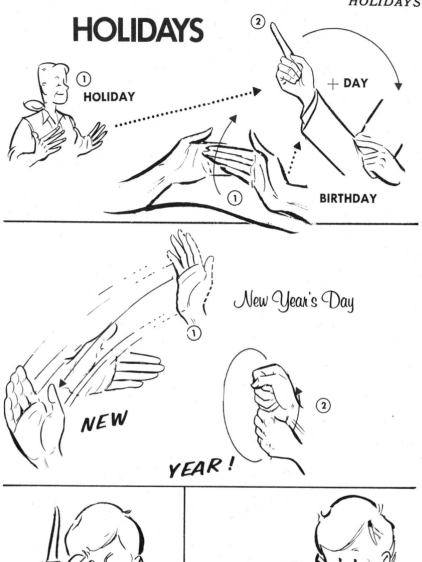

① HOLIDAY

② + DAY

① BIRTHDAY

New Year's Day

NEW

YEAR !

②

Lincoln's Birthday

Washington's Birthday

311

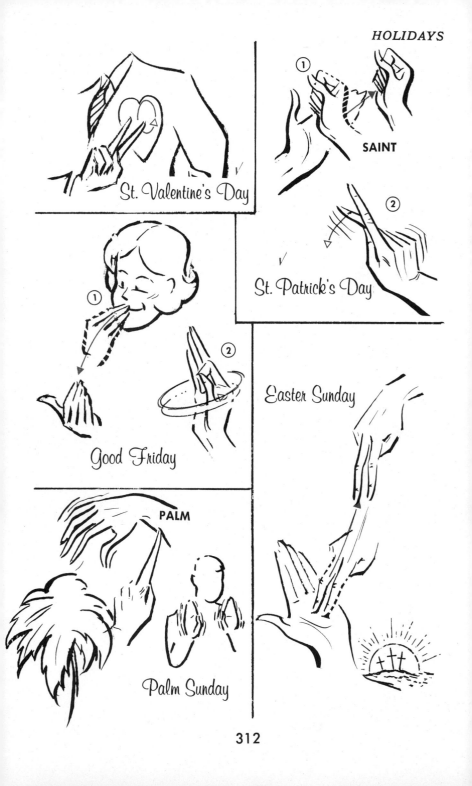

HOLIDAYS

St. Valentine's Day

SAINT

St. Patrick's Day

Good Friday

Easter Sunday

PALM

Palm Sunday

312

APRIL FOOL's DAY

Mother's Day

Father's Day

① ②
Memorial Day ✓

VETERAN'S DAY

The letter "V"

Flag Day

SOLDIER

As in holding a gun, soldier-like, against the side.

313

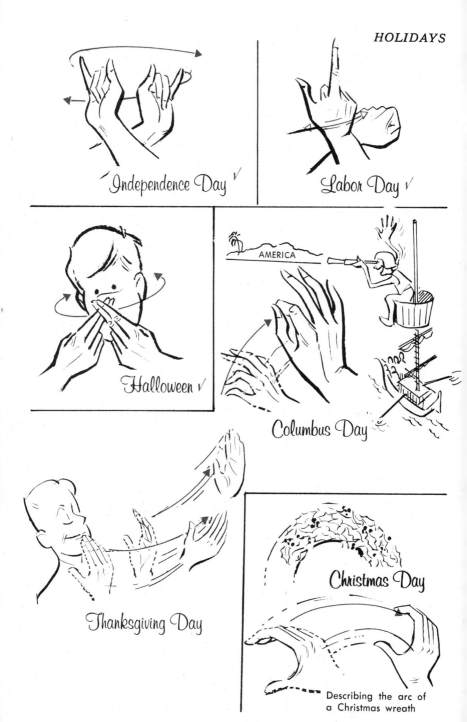

Independence Day ✓

Labor Day ✓

Halloween ✓

Columbus Day

Thanksgiving Day

Christmas Day

Describing the arc of
a Christmas wreath

314

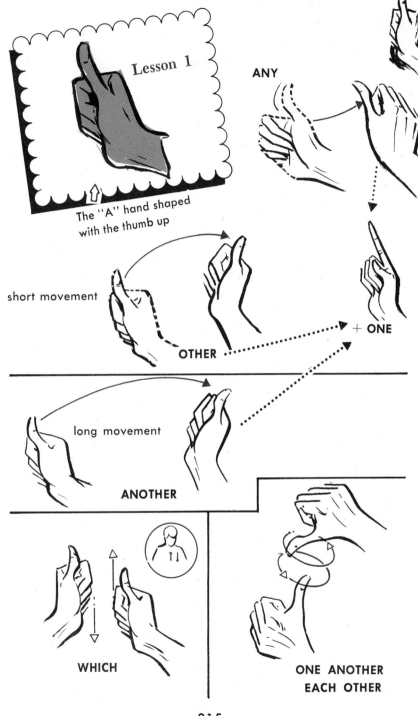

Lesson 1

The "A" hand shaped with the thumb up

ANY

short movement

OTHER

+ ONE

long movement

ANOTHER

WHICH

ONE ANOTHER
EACH OTHER

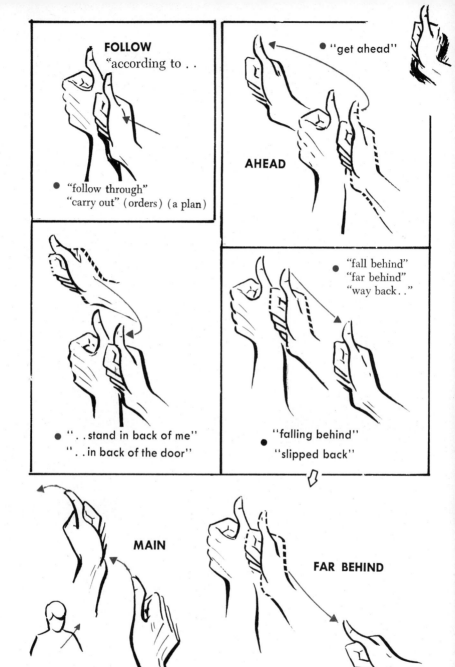

FOLLOW
"according to . .

"follow through"
"carry out" (orders) (a plan)

● "get ahead"

AHEAD

". . stand in back of me"
". . in back of the door"

"fall behind"
"far behind"
"way back . ."

"falling behind"
"slipped back"

MAIN

"The **MAIN** thing is that . . ."

FAR BEHIND

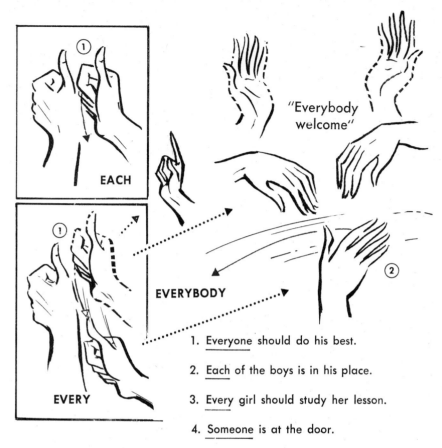

EACH

"Everybody welcome"

EVERYBODY

EVERY

"The boy stood alongside of the car"

1. Everyone should do his best.

2. Each of the boys is in his place.

3. Every girl should study her lesson.

4. Someone is at the door.

5. Neither of the girls is at home.

6. Anyone who wishes may go.

7. Each of us has a ticket and some money.

8. Several of us have tickets for the movie.

9. It seems everybody wants to go.

10. Few have read the book.

11. Some have not done their duties.

12. All of us wants to stay home.

13. Everybody is happy!

317

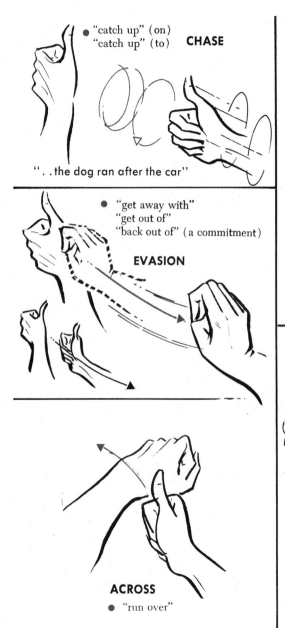

"catch up" (on)
"catch up" (to) **CHASE**

". . the dog ran after the car"

"get away with"
"get out of"
"back out of" (a commitment)

EVASION

ACROSS

"run over"

". . chumming
together"

FOLLOW UP

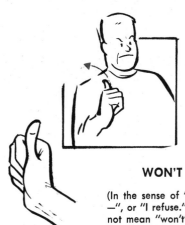

WON'T

(In the sense of "I won't —", or "I refuse." It does not mean "won't" where the word simply indicates "will not", as, "It will not rain tomorrow.")

REFUSE the letter "R"

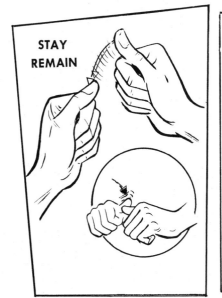

STAY
REMAIN

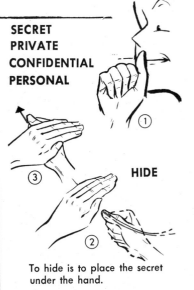

SECRET
PRIVATE
CONFIDENTIAL
PERSONAL

HIDE

To hide is to place the secret under the hand.

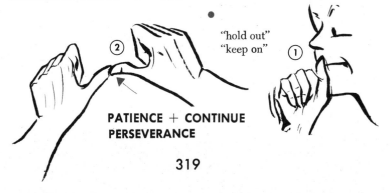

"hold out"
"keep on"

PATIENCE + CONTINUE
PERSEVERANCE

319

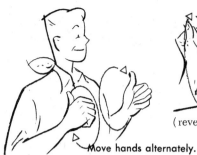

(reverse the movement for DRAMA)

Move hands alternately.

AMBITIOUS

(anxious to put oneself forward)
Bring the hand up and outward, giving
the body a sympathetic motion to indicate pushing oneself forward.

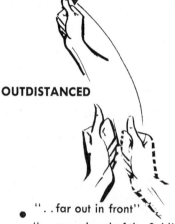

OUTDISTANCED

- "..far out in front"
  "..way ahead of the field"

PROUD
PRIDE"

Throw chest out proudly and draw the
thumb up to the center of the breast.

IMPRESSION
EMPHASIZE

- "make an impression on.."
  "good + impression"
  "bad + impression"

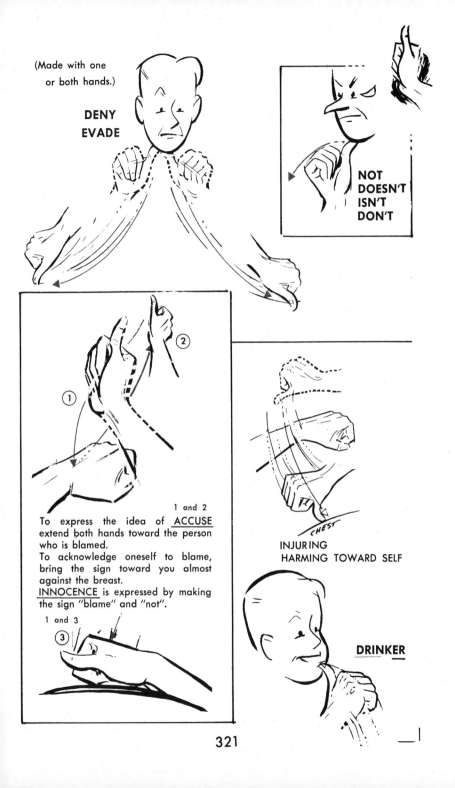

(Made with one or both hands.)

**DENY
EVADE**

**NOT
DOESN'T
ISN'T
DON'T**

1 and 2

To express the idea of <u>ACCUSE</u> extend both hands toward the person who is blamed.

To acknowledge oneself to blame, bring the sign toward you almost against the breast.

<u>INNOCENCE</u> is expressed by making the sign "blame" and "not".

1 and 3

CHEST

**INJURING
HARMING TOWARD SELF**

DRIN<u>K</u>ER

321

● **DETERIORATING**
(state of health or environment)

COAT

This sign is used for any kind of coats.

●
"put on" coat
"take off" your coat
"try on"
"hang up" your coat

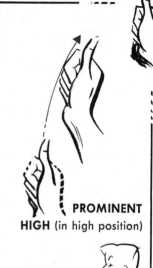

PROMINENT

HIGH (in high position)

**BASE
LOW**

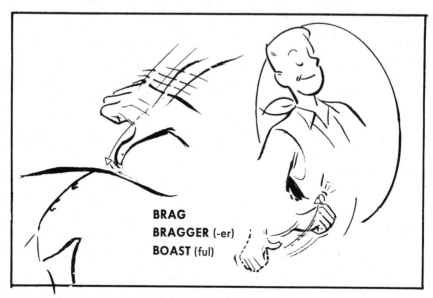

**BRAG
BRAGGER** (-er)
BOAST (ful)

322

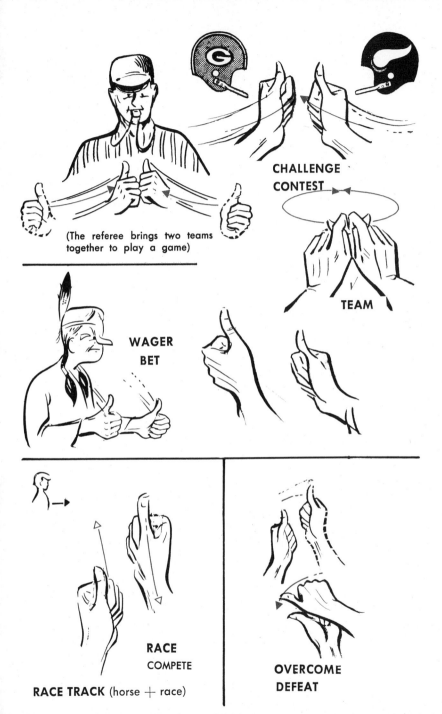

CHALLENGE
CONTEST

TEAM

(The referee brings two teams together to play a game)

WAGER
BET

RACE
COMPETE

RACE TRACK (horse + race)

OVERCOME
DEFEAT

323

BEST

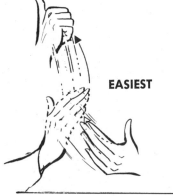

EASIEST

BETTER

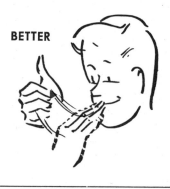

EASIER

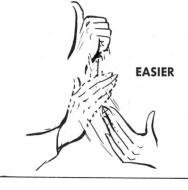

GOOD

EASY

(read upward)

BRIGHT
FAST
PRETTY
SMOOTH
CLEAN
DARK

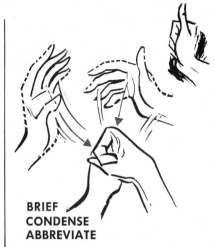

Combined with an adjective like LARGE, it means largER. Raised still higher, it means largEST.

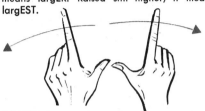

LARGE, larg<u>er</u>, larg<u>est</u>

BRIEF CONDENSE ABBREVIATE

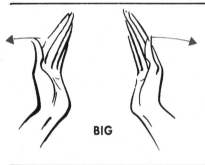

BIG

SMALL

LITTLE

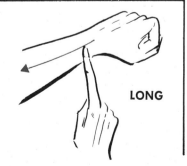

SHORT

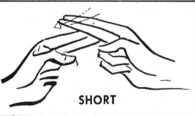

LONG

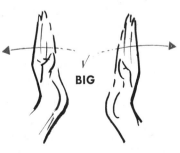

BIG

325

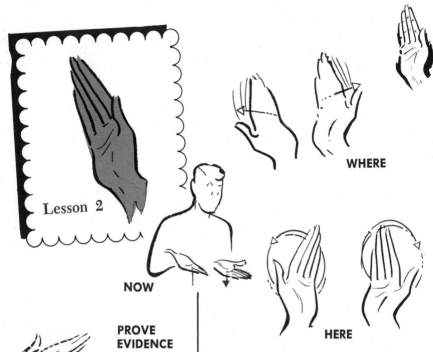

Lesson 2

NOW

WHERE

HERE

PROVE
EVIDENCE

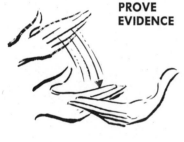

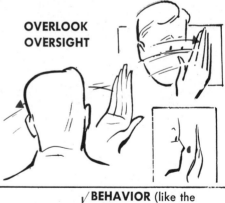

OVERLOOK
OVERSIGHT

SLOW

"take it easy"
● "slow down" (and rest)

Move slowly down the back
of the left hand.

✓ BEHAVIOR (like the
"do" sign)

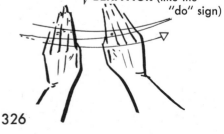

326

PREVENT

"The cold 'kept' me from enjoying myself."

STOP

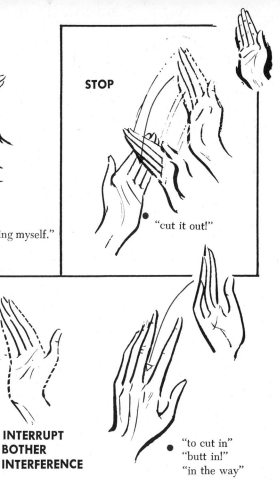

"cut it out!"

INTERRUPT
BOTHER
INTERFERENCE

"to cut in"
"butt in!"
"in the way"

CHAT

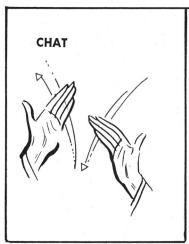

SPEECH
LECTURE

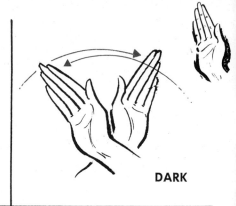

● "clean out" "get rid of" **CLEAN**

DARK

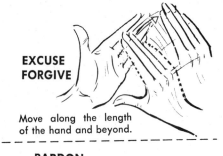

EXCUSE FORGIVE

Move along the length of the hand and beyond.

LAID OFF

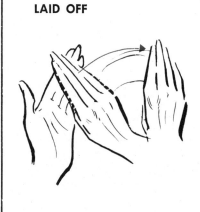

PARDON

Rub back and forth on palm.

SCHOOL

RIGHT

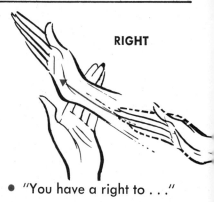

● "You have a right to . . ."

328

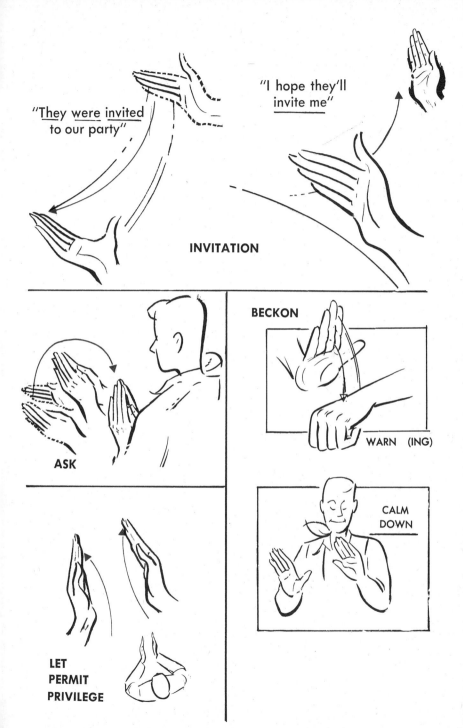

"They were invited to our party"

"I hope they'll invite me"

INVITATION

ASK

BECKON

WARN (ING)

CALM DOWN

LET
PERMIT
PRIVILEGE

329

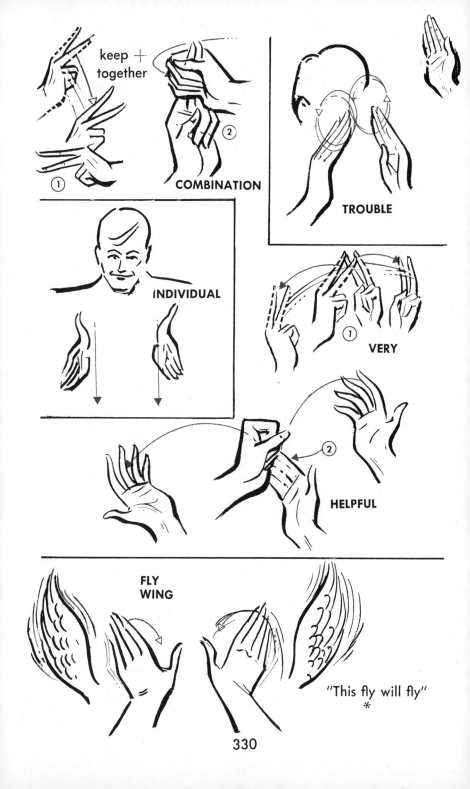

keep + together

COMBINATION

TROUBLE

INDIVIDUAL

VERY

HELPFUL

FLY WING

"This fly will fly"
*

330

BECOME

● "get sick" sign: become + sick
  "get wet"   become + wet

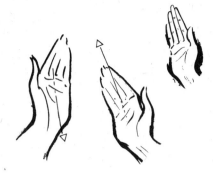

SERVICE
SERVE

FILL

FULL

ENOUGH
PLENTY

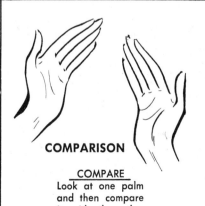

AGAINST

COMPARISON

COMPARE
Look at one palm
and then compare
it with the other
palm several times.

331

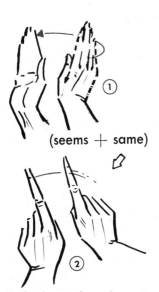

(seems + same)

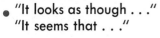

• "It looks as though . . ."
"It seems that . . ."

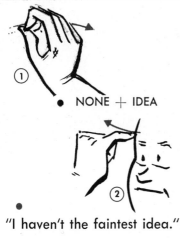

• NONE + IDEA

• "I haven't the faintest idea."

• ". . . for instance"

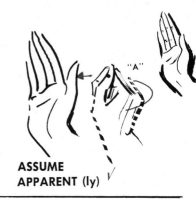

**ASSUME
APPARENT (ly)**

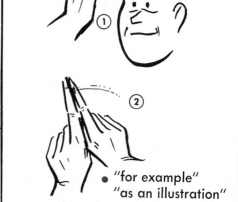

• "for example"
"as an illustration"

"John looks just like
his Uncle"

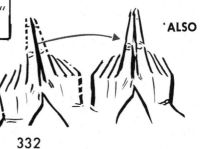

·**ALSO**

332

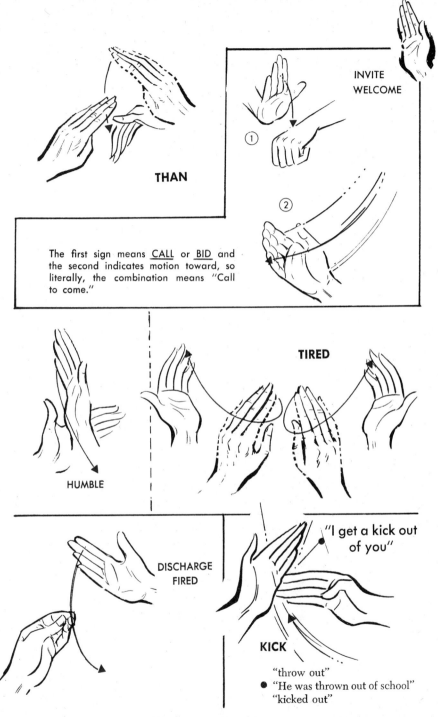

THAN

INVITE WELCOME

① ②

The first sign means <u>CALL</u> or <u>BID</u> and the second indicates motion toward, so literally, the combination means "Call to come."

TIRED

HUMBLE

DISCHARGE FIRED

"I get a kick out of you"

KICK

"throw out"
● "He was thrown out of school"
"kicked out"

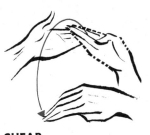

**CHEAP
BARGAIN**

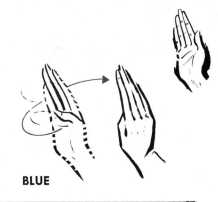

BLUE

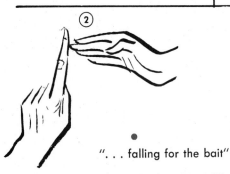

". . . falling for the bait"

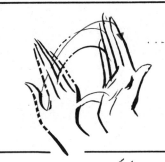

DEADLINE

WAY

"W" for **WAY**
"R" for **ROAD**
"M" for **METHOD**

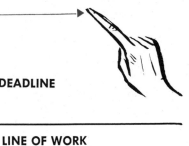

**LINE OF WORK
SPECIALIST**

**MAJOR
SUBJECT**

"to be in charge of.."   responsible + for
"to have charge of"   control + of

DUTY

√ <u>B</u>URDEN

    letter "R" for
√ <u>R</u>ESPONSIBILITY
    "F" for
√ <u>F</u>AULT

**HELP
ASSISTANCE
AID
BENEFIT**

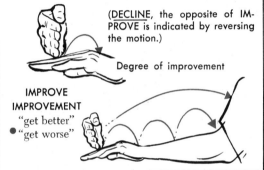

(<u>DECLINE</u>, the opposite of IM-
PROVE is indicated by reversing
the motion.)

Degree of improvement

**IMPROVE
IMPROVEMENT**
    "get better"
● "get worse"

**HOPE
EXPECT
ANTICIPATE**

INDIFFERENCE

    Brush left hand one way with palm
    and then back with back of hand.
    Repeat several times.

       "it makes no difference"
    ● "never mind"
       "anyway"

335

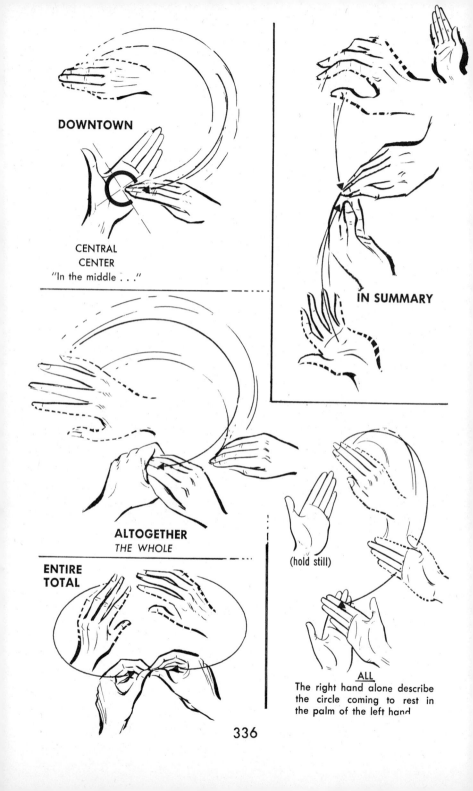

DOWNTOWN

CENTRAL
CENTER
"In the middle . . ."

IN SUMMARY

ALTOGETHER
THE WHOLE

(hold still)

**ENTIRE
TOTAL**

<u>ALL</u>
The right hand alone describe
the circle coming to rest in
the palm of the left hand

336

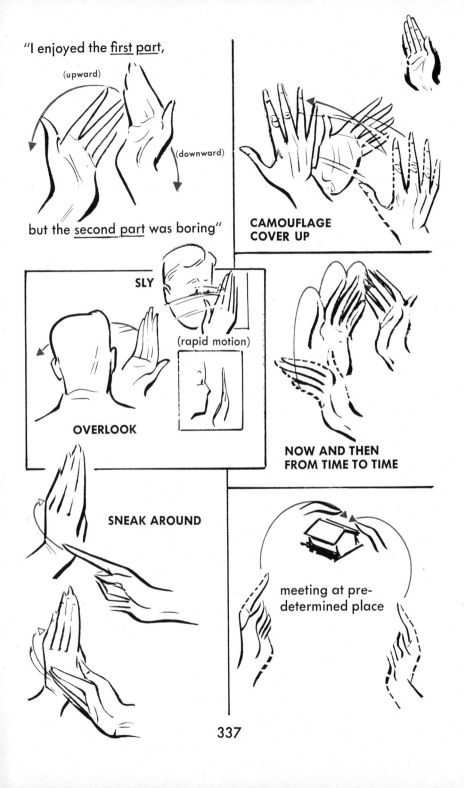

"I enjoyed the <u>first part</u>,

(upward)

(downward)

but the <u>second part</u> was boring"

CAMOUFLAGE COVER UP

SLY

(rapid motion)

OVERLOOK

NOW AND THEN FROM TIME TO TIME

SNEAK AROUND

meeting at predetermined place

Lesson 3

**START
BEGIN
INITIATE**

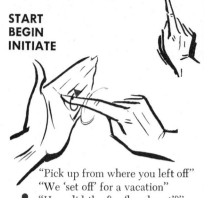

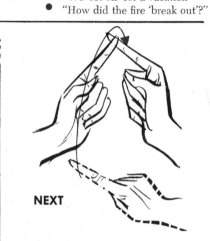

"Pick up from where you left off"
"We 'set off' for a vacation"
• "How did the fire 'break out'?"

FIRST

NEXT

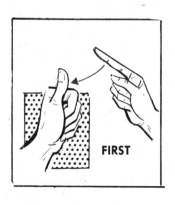

FIRST

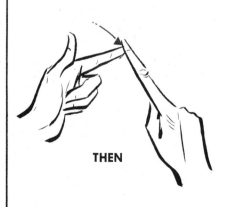

THEN

338

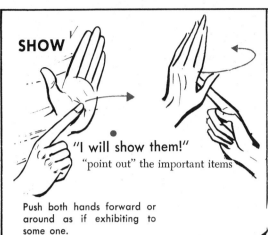

SHOW

"I will show them!"
"point out" the important items

Push both hands forward or around as if exhibiting to some one.

SAMPLE

DEMONSTRATE

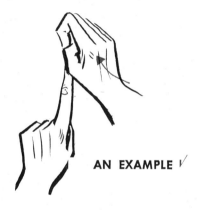

AN EXAMPLE

SYMBOL

ILLUSTRATE

RISING
SUCCEEDING
also means **TALL**

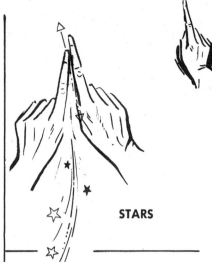

STARS

ARGUE
ARGUMENT
DEBATE

● "That's correct"
"That's right"

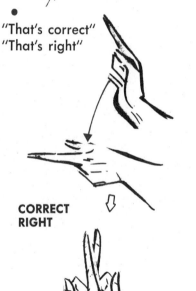

CORRECT
RIGHT

● *"RIGHT ON!"*

move both hands
outward

340

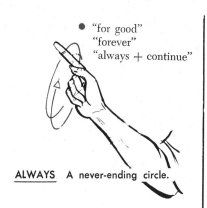

● "for good"
  "forever"
  "always + continue"

ALWAYS A never-ending circle.

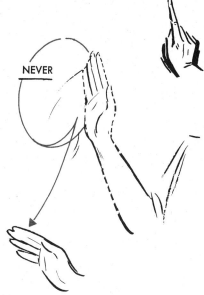

NEVER

Opposite to ALWAYS. This shows a circle that is broken off.

STILL (CONTINUING)

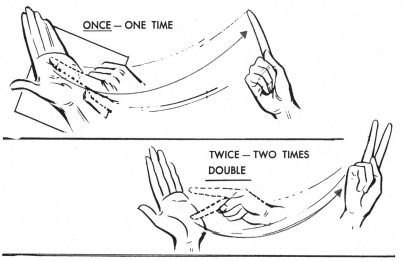

ONCE — ONE TIME

TWICE — TWO TIMES
DOUBLE

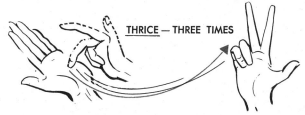

THRICE — THREE TIMES

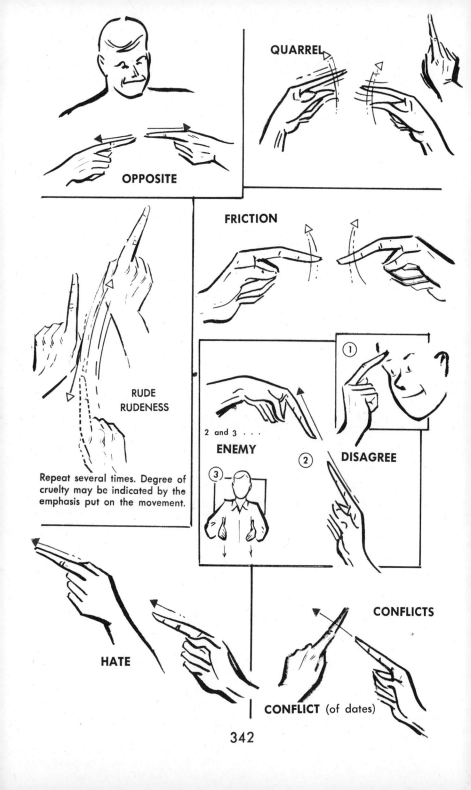

OPPOSITE

QUARREL

FRICTION

RUDE
RUDENESS

Repeat several times. Degree of
cruelty may be indicated by the
emphasis put on the movement.

2 and 3 . . .
ENEMY

①

②

③

DISAGREE

HATE

CONFLICTS

CONFLICT (of dates)

342

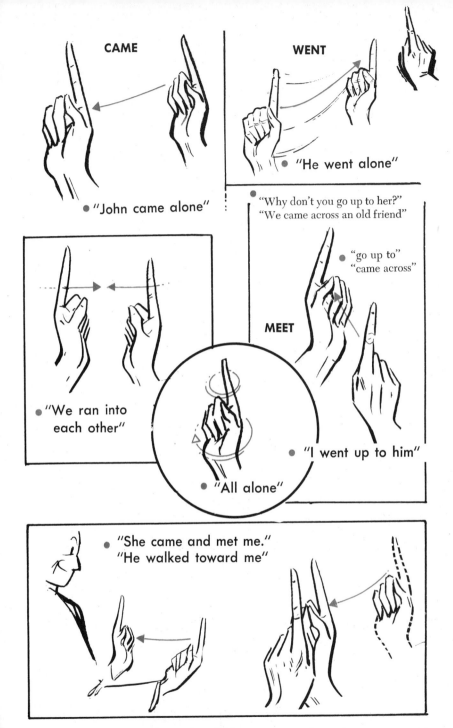

CAME

"John came alone"

WENT

"He went alone"

"Why don't you go up to her?"
"We came across an old friend"

"go up to"
"came across"

MEET

"We ran into each other"

"All alone"

"I went up to him"

"She came and met me."
"He walked toward me"

343

MEET

● "I went up to her,
but she brushed me off."

FRUSTRATION
(A slap in the face!)

● "If I were popular,
I would be mobbed!"

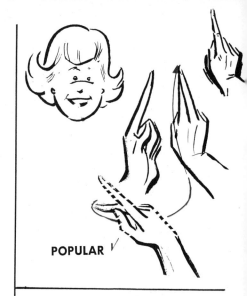

POPULAR

SURROUND

● "She was surrounded with boys"
"The boys gathered around Mary"

MOBBED

● "Mary was mobbed as she walked in"

344

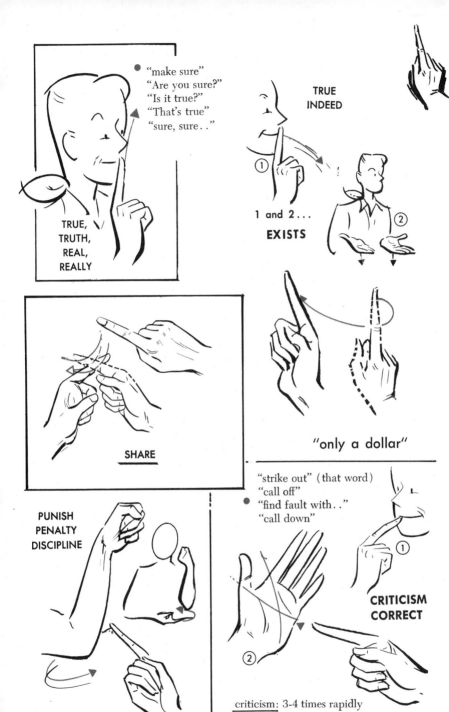

"make sure"
"Are you sure?"
"Is it true?"
"That's true"
"sure, sure.."

TRUE,
TRUTH,
REAL,
REALLY

TRUE
INDEED

1 and 2...
EXISTS

SHARE

"only a dollar"

**PUNISH
PENALTY
DISCIPLINE**

"strike out" (that word)
"call off"
"find fault with.."
"call down"

**CRITICISM
CORRECT**

criticism: 3-4 times rapidly

345

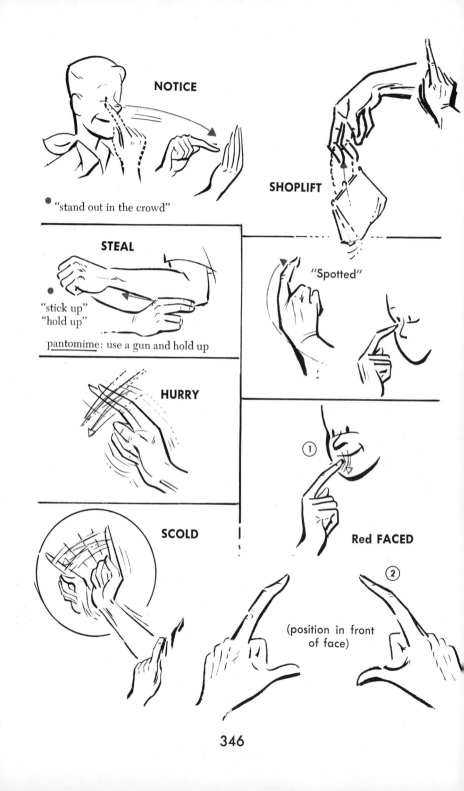

NOTICE

"stand out in the crowd"

SHOPLIFT

"Spotted"

STEAL

"stick up"
"hold up"

pantomime: use a gun and hold up

HURRY

SCOLD

① Red **FACED**

(position in front
of face)

②

"Tell me . . ."
"Told me . . ."

"Tell him . . ."
"Told him (them) . . ."

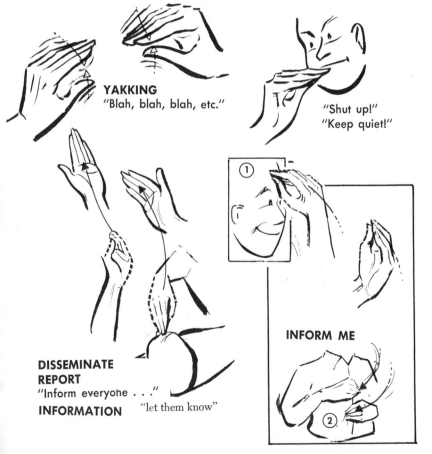

YAKKING
"Blah, blah, blah, etc."

"Shut up!"
"Keep quiet!"

**DISSEMINATE
REPORT**
"Inform everyone . . ."
INFORMATION "let them know"

INFORM ME

347

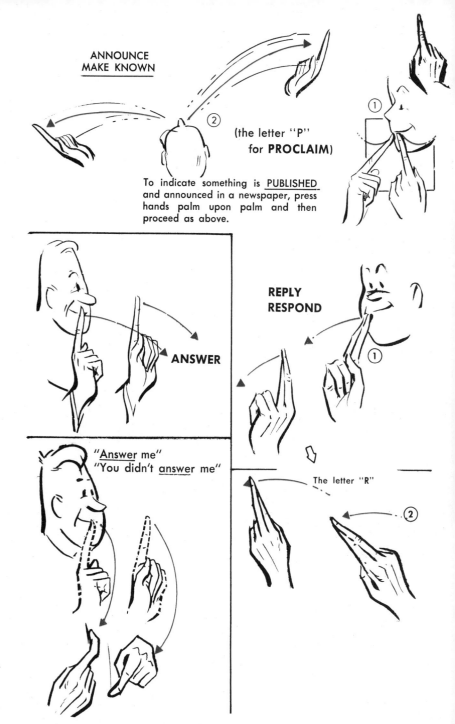

ANNOUNCE
MAKE KNOWN

②

(the letter "P"
for **PROCLAIM**)

①

To indicate something is PUBLISHED and announced in a newspaper, press hands palm upon palm and then proceed as above.

REPLY
RESPOND

ANSWER

①

"Answer me"
"You didn't answer me"

The letter "R"

②

348

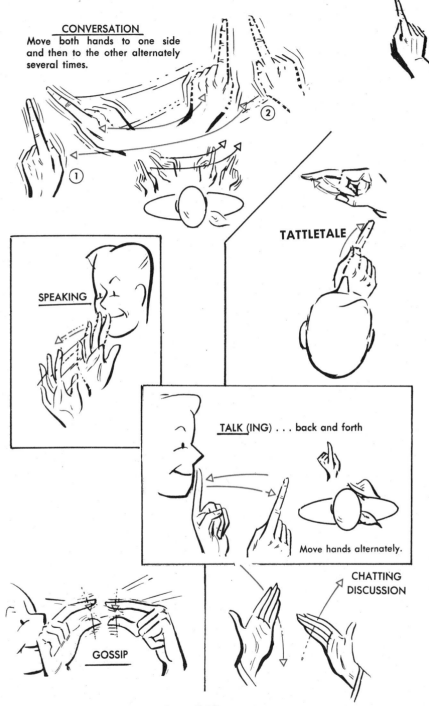

CONVERSATION
Move both hands to one side and then to the other alternately several times.

① ②

TATTLETALE

SPEAKING

TALK (ING) . . . back and forth
Move hands alternately.

CHATTING
DISCUSSION

GOSSIP

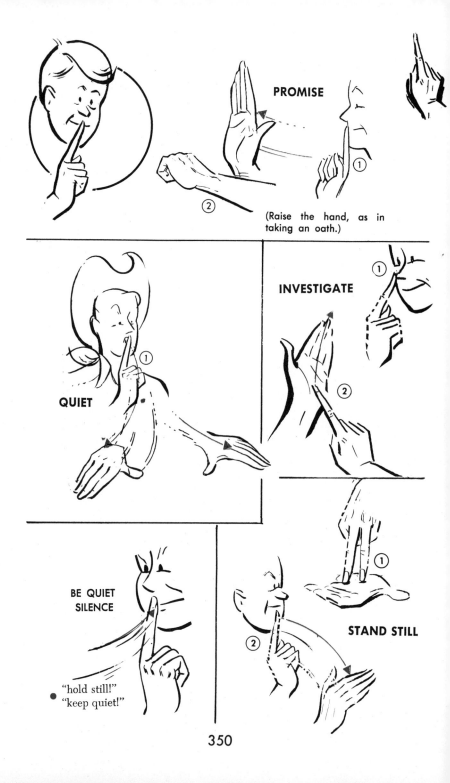

PROMISE

(Raise the hand, as in taking an oath.)

INVESTIGATE

QUIET

BE QUIET
SILENCE

"hold still!"
"keep quiet!"

STAND STILL

350

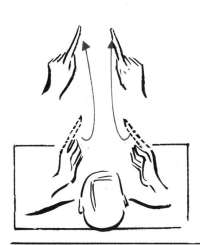

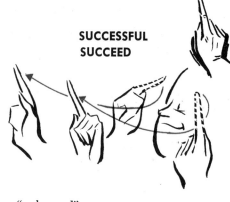

SUCCESSFUL
SUCCEED

- "make good"
  "How did you make out in school?"

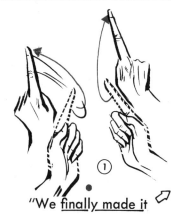

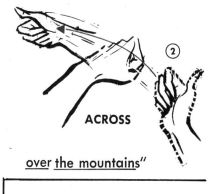

ACROSS

over the mountains"

"We finally made it

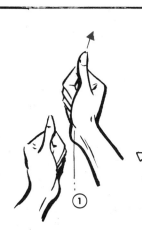

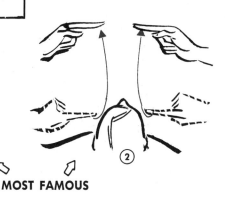

MOST FAMOUS

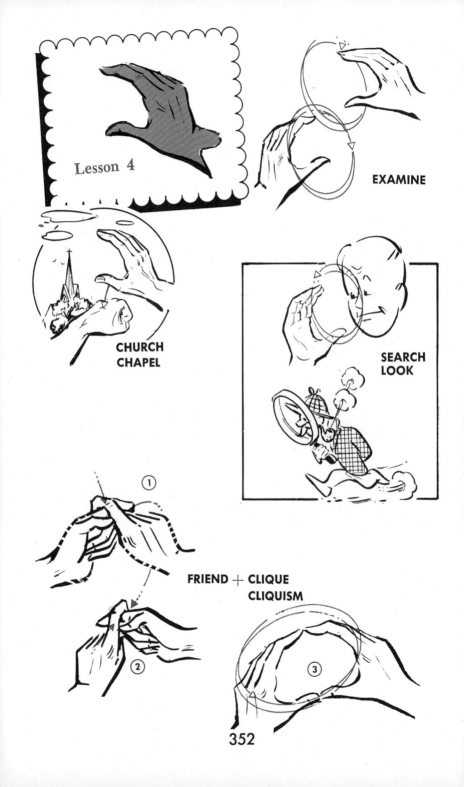

Lesson 4

EXAMINE

CHURCH
CHAPEL

SEARCH
LOOK

① ②

FRIEND + CLIQUE
CLIQUISM

③

352

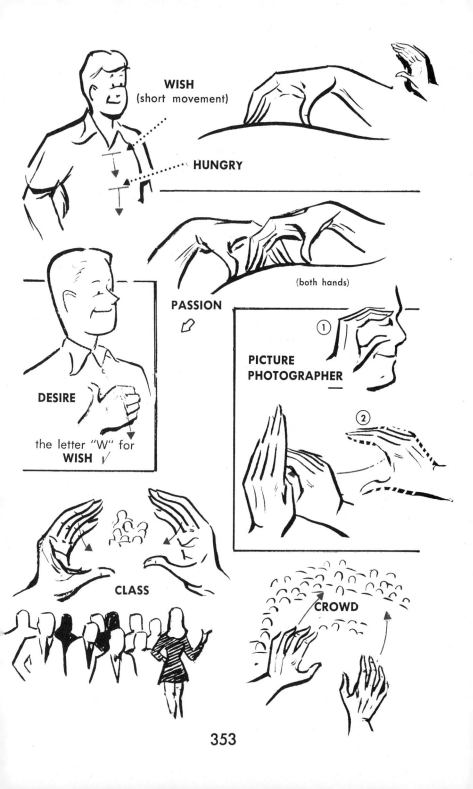

WISH
(short movement)

HUNGRY

PASSION

(both hands)

DESIRE

the letter "W" for
WISH

**PICTURE
PHOTOGRAPHER**

①

②

CLASS

CROWD

353

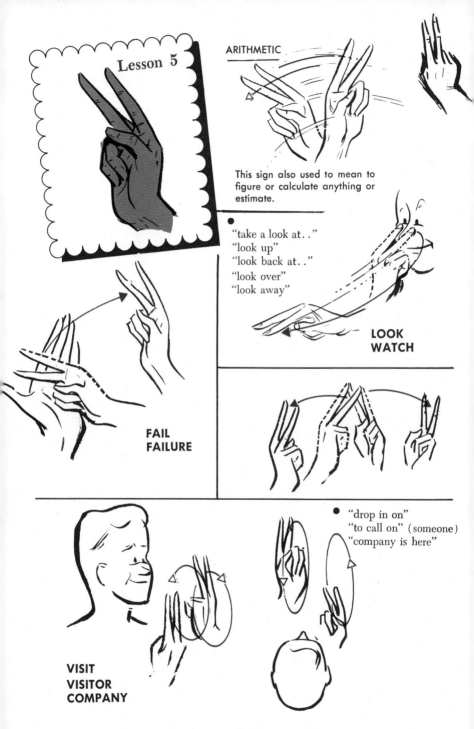

Lesson 5

ARITHMETIC

This sign also used to mean to figure or calculate anything or estimate.

• "take a look at.."
"look up"
"look back at.."
"look over"
"look away"

**LOOK
WATCH**

**FAIL
FAILURE**

• "drop in on"
"to call on" (someone)
"company is here"

**VISIT
VISITOR
COMPANY**

354

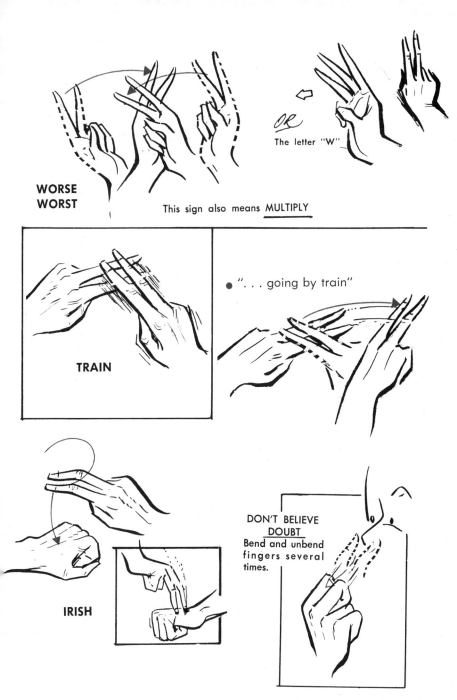

The letter "W"

WORSE
WORST

This sign also means <u>MULTIPLY</u>

TRAIN

"... going by train"

IRISH

DON'T BELIEVE
DOUBT
Bend and unbend
fingers several
times.

355

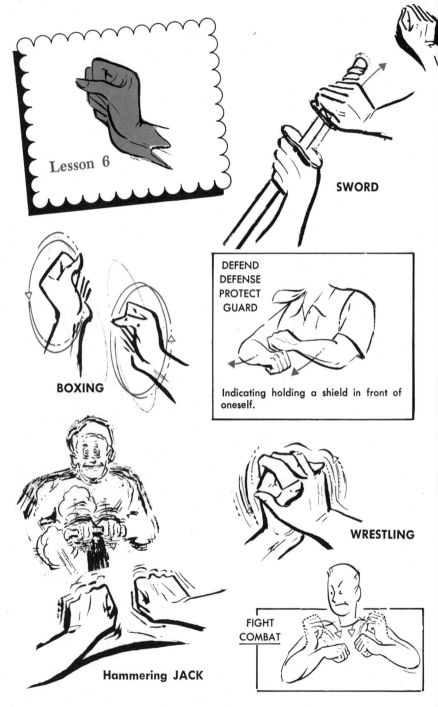

Lesson 6

SWORD

BOXING

DEFEND
DEFENSE
PROTECT
GUARD

Indicating holding a shield in front of oneself.

WRESTLING

Hammering JACK

FIGHT
COMBAT

WORK (ING)

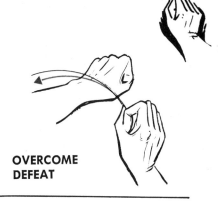

**OVERCOME
DEFEAT**

SLAVE

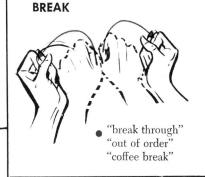

BREAK

- "break through"
  "out of order"
  "coffee break"

LOCK

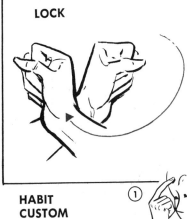

**HABIT
CUSTOM**

① ②

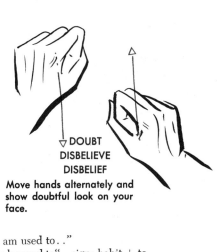

▽ **DOUBT
DISBELIEVE
DISBELIEF**

**Move hands alternately and
show doubtful look on your
face.**

- "I am used to.."
  "to be used to"   sign: habit + to
  "get used to"

357

GIVE UP
LOSE HOPE
DISCOURAGED

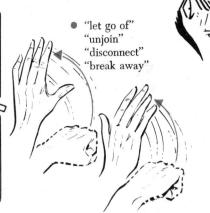

● "let go of"
"unjoin"
"disconnect"
"break away"

Simultaneously with the action draw the head and shoulders back somewhat.

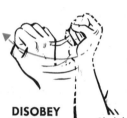

**DISOBEY
STRIKE
REVOLT
REBELLION**

Slightly turning the head to indicate defiance.

OBEY

Some carry the hands up toward right shoulder and drop from there.

SPONSOR

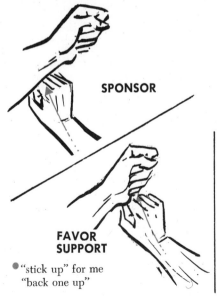

**FAVOR
SUPPORT**

● "stick up" for me
"back one up"

DIFFICULT

Circle one around the other, moving both at the same time. Make a show of some effort in moving the hands.

358

Lesson 7

"get in touch with.."
"get in contact with.."
"We have been in all
parts of the country"
(finish + contact)

**TOUCH
CONTACT**

● "take pity on"
"feel sorry for"

"I pity you"

Stroking motion of the hand, as if giving comforts to an imaginary object of pity.

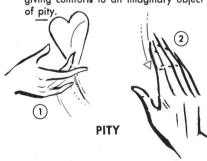

① ②

PITY

REFERENCE TO THE HEART:

FEEL

TOUCH

HEART

(draw the shape of heart on chest)

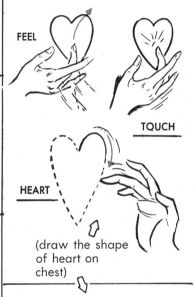

359

EMPTY
VACANT

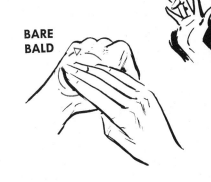

BARE
BALD

NAKED

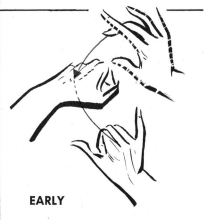

EARLY

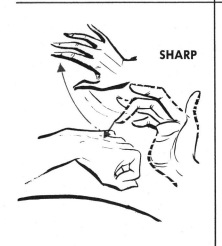

SHARP

DELICIOUS

360

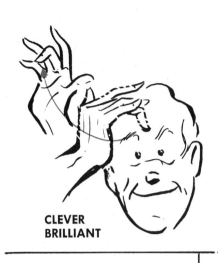

**CLEVER
BRILLIANT**

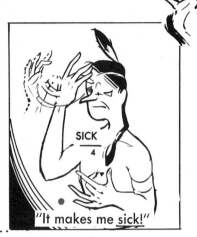

SICK
4

"It makes me <u>sick!</u>"

**SICK
ILL**

"My mind is <u>blank</u>"

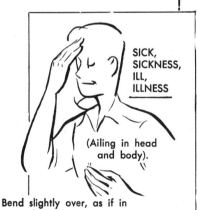

SICK,
SICKNESS,
ILL,
ILLNESS

(Ailing in head
and body).

Bend slightly over, as if in
some distress.

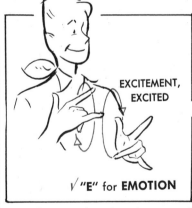

EXCITEMENT,
EXCITED

√ **"E"** for **EMOTION**

Draw first one then the other upward
against the body and repeat, moving the
hands alternately, assuming a nervous
manner.

361

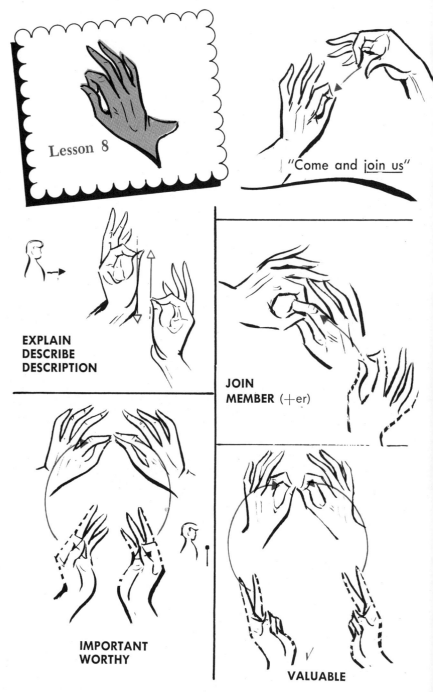

Lesson 8

"Come and join us"

EXPLAIN
DESCRIBE
DESCRIPTION

JOIN
MEMBER (+er)

IMPORTANT
WORTHY

VALUABLE

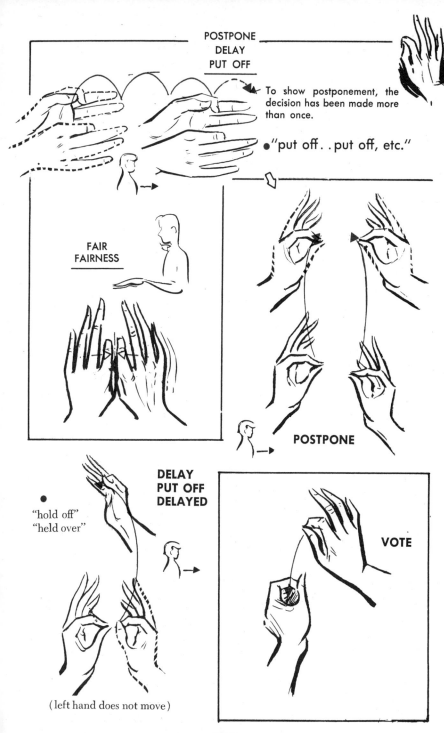

POSTPONE
DELAY
PUT OFF

To show postponement, the decision has been made more than once.

● "put off . . put off, etc."

FAIR
FAIRNESS

POSTPONE

DELAY
PUT OFF
DELAYED

●
"hold off"
"held over"

VOTE

(left hand does not move)

363

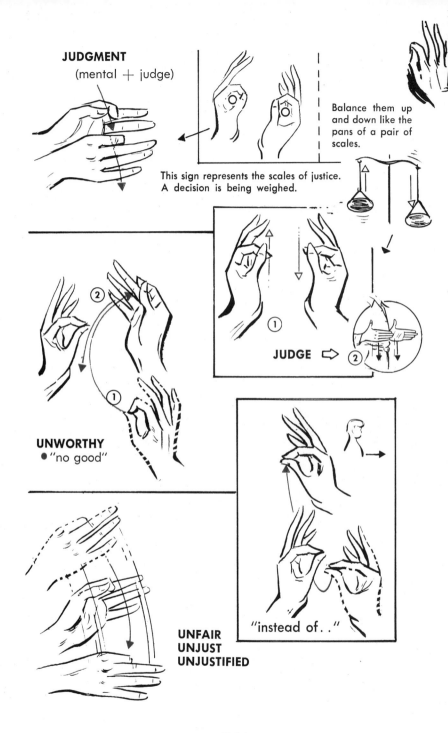

JUDGMENT
(mental + judge)

Balance them up and down like the pans of a pair of scales.

This sign represents the scales of justice. A decision is being weighed.

JUDGE ⇨

UNWORTHY
● "no good"

"instead of.."

**UNFAIR
UNJUST
UNJUSTIFIED**

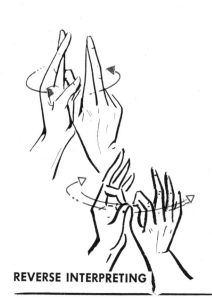

REVERSE INTERPRETING

RAPPORT
BELONG
- "stick together"

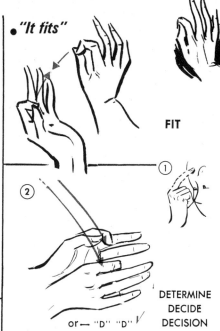

- *"It fits"*

FIT

② ①

DETERMINE
DECIDE
DECISION

or — "D" "D"

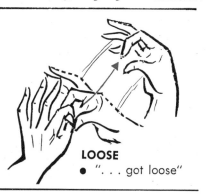

LOOSE
- ". . . got loose"

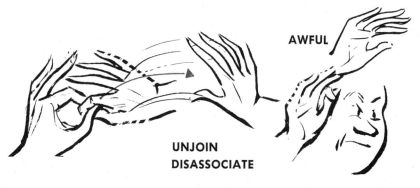

AWFUL

UNJOIN
DISASSOCIATE

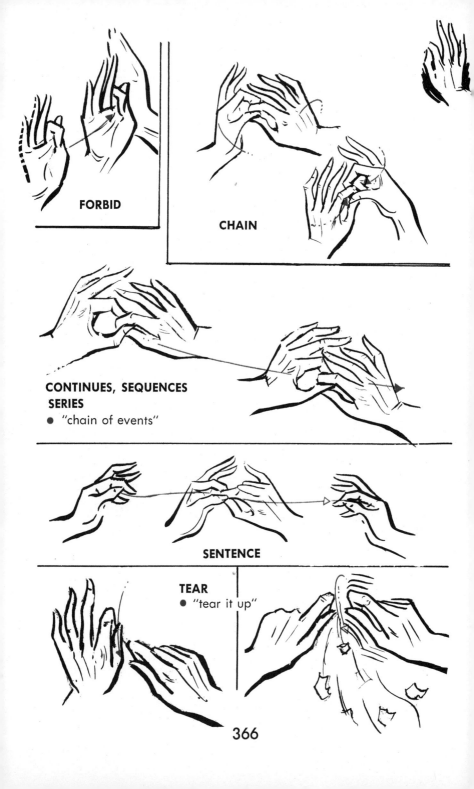

FORBID

CHAIN

CONTINUES, SEQUENCES SERIES
- "chain of events"

SENTENCE

TEAR
- "tear it up"

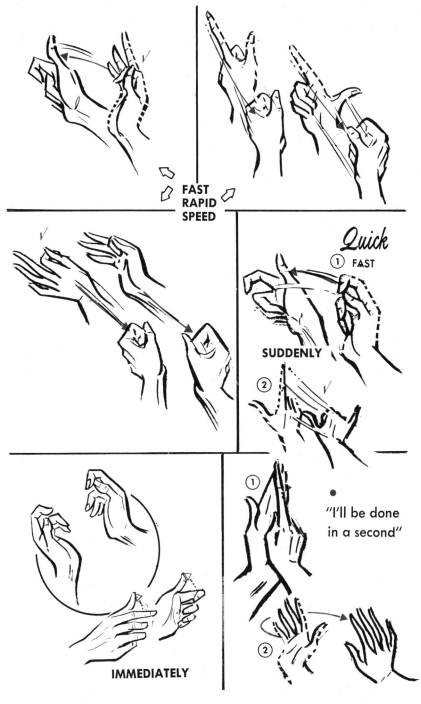

FAST
RAPID
SPEED

Quick
① FAST

SUDDENLY

②

IMMEDIATELY

①

②

● "I'll be done in a second"

SLOW
Move slowly down the back
of the left hand.

HURRY
give it an up-and-down motion
Use both hands.

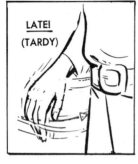

LATE!
(TARDY)

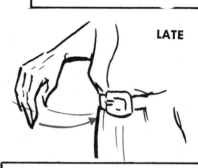

LATE

HUSTLING
ALERT

LAZY
LAZINESS

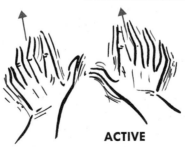

ACTIVE

368

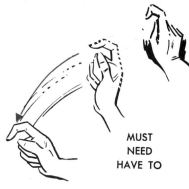

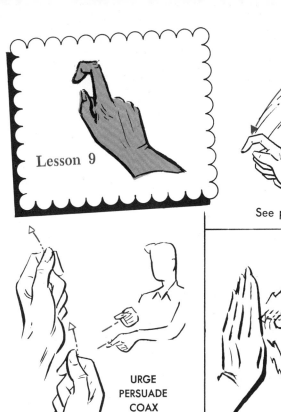

Lesson 9

MUST
NEED
HAVE TO

See page 126, 127

URGE
PERSUADE
COAX
PERSUASION

BATTERY √

Push hands out and draw back quickly, repeating the motion several times.

the letter "R" for
REQUEST

①

REQUIRE
DEMAND

②

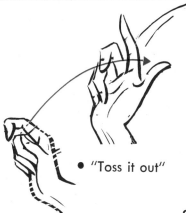

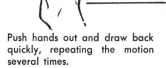

● "Toss it out"

Draw the hand back quickly.

369

FROM

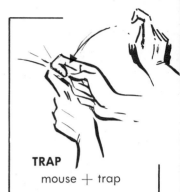

TRAP

mouse + trap

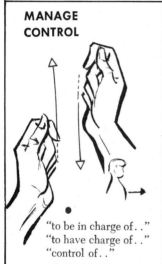

**MANAGE
CONTROL**

"to be in charge of.."
"to have charge of.."
"control of.."

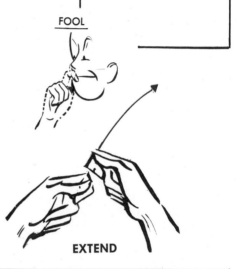

FOOL

EXTEND

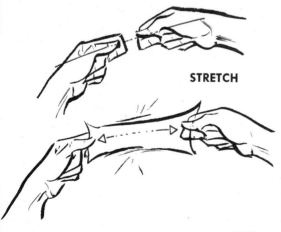

STRETCH

**CHARGE
FINE**

370

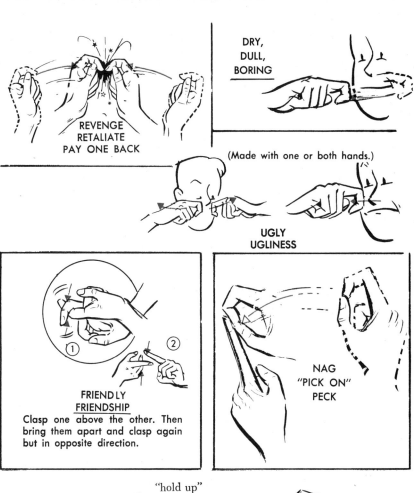

REVENGE
RETALIATE
PAY ONE BACK

DRY,
DULL,
BORING

(Made with one or both hands.)

UGLY
UGLINESS

FRIENDLY
FRIENDSHIP
Clasp one above the other. Then
bring them apart and clasp again
but in opposite direction.

NAG
"PICK ON"
PECK

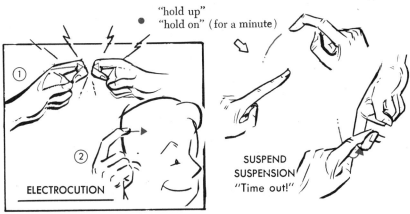

"hold up"
"hold on" (for a minute)

ELECTROCUTION

SUSPEND
SUSPENSION
"Time out!"

371

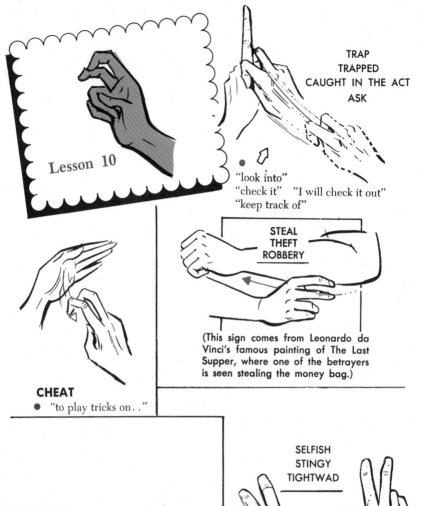

Lesson 10

TRAP
TRAPPED
CAUGHT IN THE ACT
ASK

"look into"
"check it"   "I will check it out"
"keep track of"

STEAL
THEFT
ROBBERY

(This sign comes from Leonardo da
Vinci's famous painting of The Last
Supper, where one of the betrayers
is seen stealing the money bag.)

CHEAT
● "to play tricks on.."

SELFISH
STINGY
TIGHTWAD

(RESTLESSNESS)

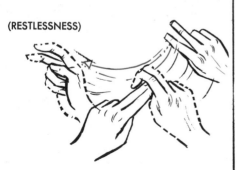

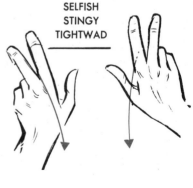

372

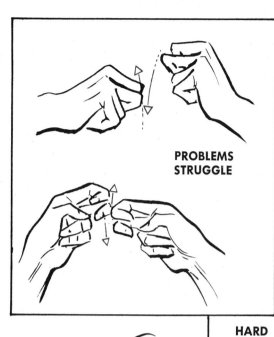

**PROBLEMS
STRUGGLE**

● $200.00

● $300.00

**HARD
TOUGH**
● **HARDBOILED**

HARDSHIP

Rub them across one way and then the other in effort to push one beyond the other.

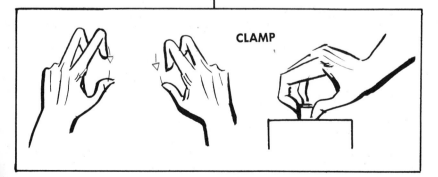

CLAMP

373

Lesson 11

FOOD

OUT
EXIT

IN
INTO

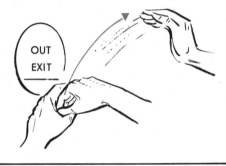

"Return it"

SEND ME

"Send it to me"

374

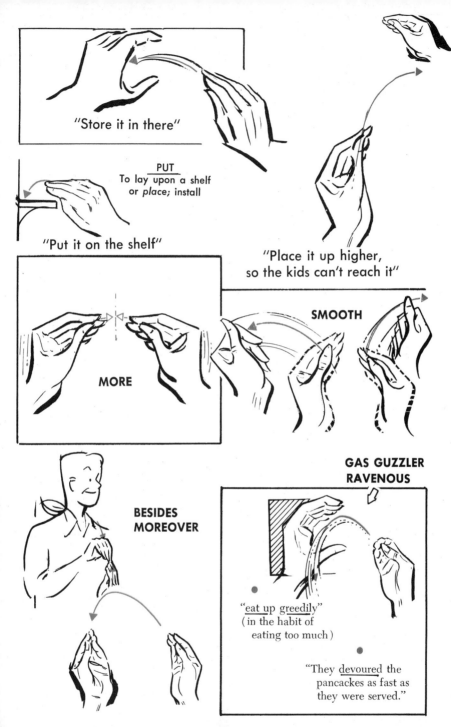

"Store it in there"

PUT
To lay upon a shelf
or *place;* install

"Put it on the shelf"

"Place it up higher,
so the kids can't reach it"

MORE

SMOOTH

BESIDES
MOREOVER

GAS GUZZLER
RAVENOUS

"eat up greedily"
(in the habit of
eating too much)

"They devoured the
pancackes as fast as
they were served."

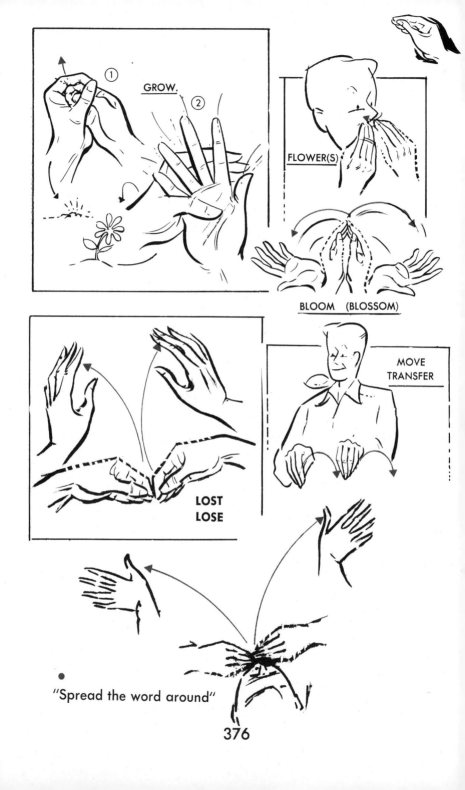

GROW.

FLOWER(S)

BLOOM (BLOSSOM)

LOST
LOSE

MOVE
TRANSFER

"Spread the word around"

376

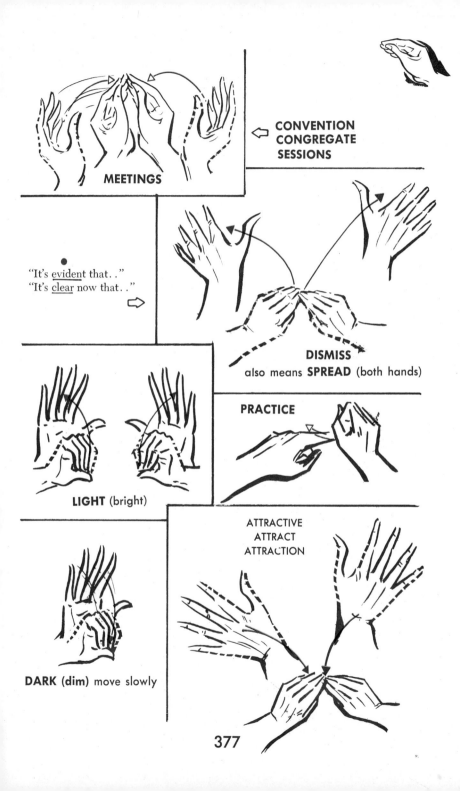

CONVENTION
CONGREGATE
SESSIONS

MEETINGS

"It's evident that.."
"It's clear now that.."

DISMISS
also means SPREAD (both hands)

PRACTICE

LIGHT (bright)

ATTRACTIVE
ATTRACT
ATTRACTION

DARK (dim) move slowly

377

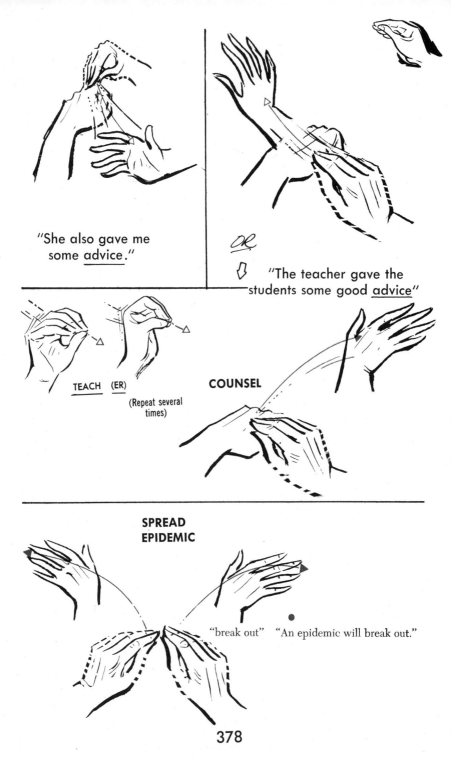

"She also gave me some <u>advice</u>."

<u>OR</u>

"The teacher gave the students some good <u>advice</u>"

<u>TEACH</u> (ER)

(Repeat several times)

COUNSEL

SPREAD EPIDEMIC

"break out"   "An epidemic will break out."

378

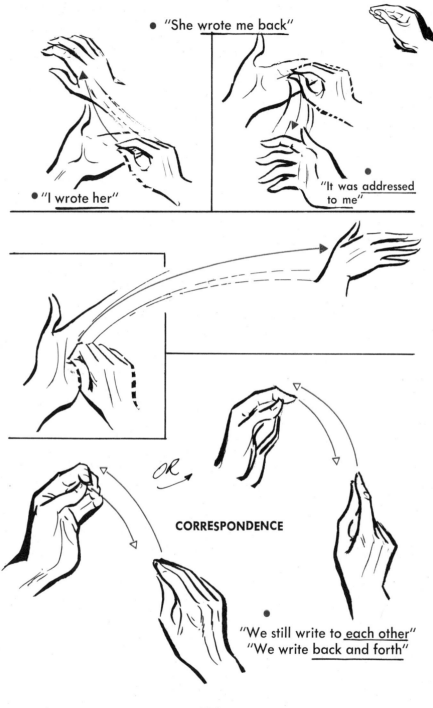

- "She wrote me back"

- "I wrote her"

- "It was addressed to me"

OR

CORRESPONDENCE

- "We still write to each other"
"We write back and forth"

379

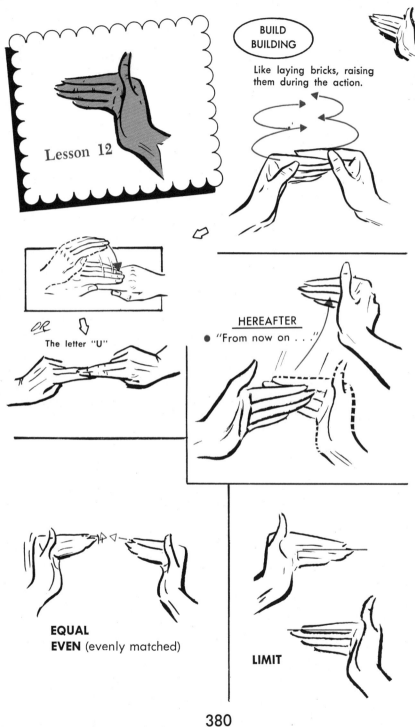

Lesson 12

BUILD
BUILDING

Like laying bricks, raising
them during the action.

OR

The letter "U"

HEREAFTER
● "From now on . . ."

EQUAL
EVEN (evenly matched)

LIMIT

380

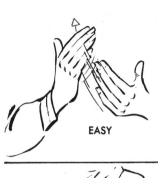

EASY

ARRIVE

- "get to" a place   sign: arrive
  "get back from"   (arrive + from)

BEFORE (place)

- "just short of . . ."
  "shy of a first down"

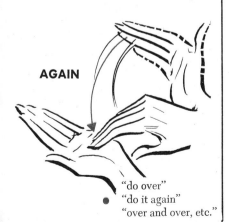

AGAIN

- "do over"
  "do it again"
  "over and over, etc."

The sign for <u>AGAIN</u> repeated two or three times.

<u>OFTEN</u>

Literally, "again and again".

FREQUENTLY

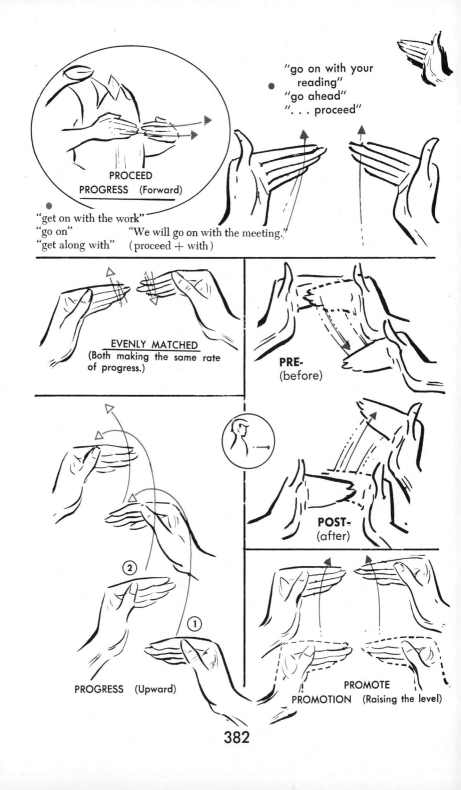

"go on with your
reading"
"go ahead"
". . . proceed"

PROCEED
PROGRESS (Forward)

"get on with the work"
"go on"   "We will go on with the meeting."
"get along with"   (proceed + with)

EVENLY MATCHED
(Both making the same rate
of progress.)

PRE-
(before)

PROGRESS (Upward)

POST-
(after)

PROMOTE
PROMOTION (Raising the level)

382

NEAREST

NEARER

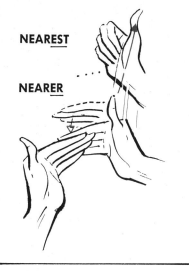

FARTHEST

FARTHER

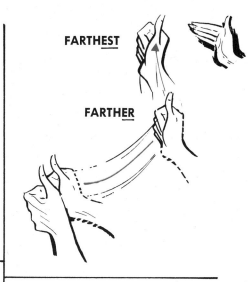

BEYOND

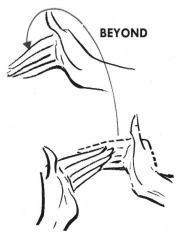

APPROACH (ING)
NEAR
CLOSE

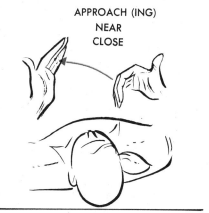

(move upward slowly)

NEXT (the other side)

"the next door neighbor"

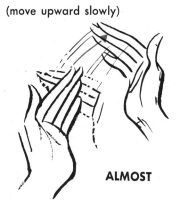

ALMOST

383

"... remind me"
(poke + remember)

PROD

ghost

"Say, did you <u>want</u> to <u>see</u> me?"

"The boys <u>took off</u>
in a great <u>hurry</u>"

384

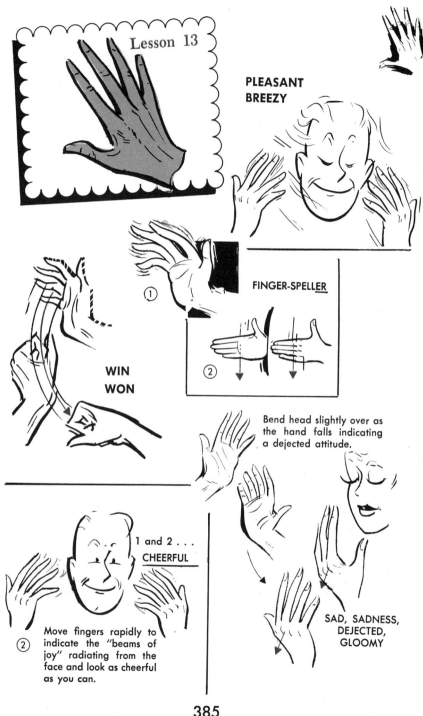

Lesson 13

PLEASANT BREEZY

FINGER-SPELLER

① ②

WIN WON

Bend head slightly over as the hand falls indicating a dejected attitude.

1 and 2 . . .
CHEERFUL

② Move fingers rapidly to indicate the "beams of joy" radiating from the face and look as cheerful as you can.

SAD, SADNESS, DEJECTED, GLOOMY

385

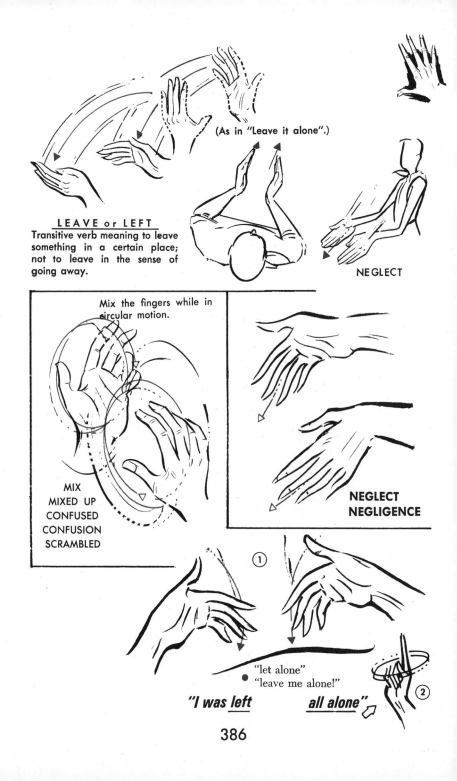

(As in "Leave it alone".)

LEAVE or LEFT
Transitive verb meaning to leave something in a certain place; not to leave in the sense of going away.

NEGLECT

Mix the fingers while in circular motion.

MIX
MIXED UP
CONFUSED
CONFUSION
SCRAMBLED

NEGLECT
NEGLIGENCE

①

● "let alone"
  "leave me alone!"

"I was left   *all alone"*

②

386

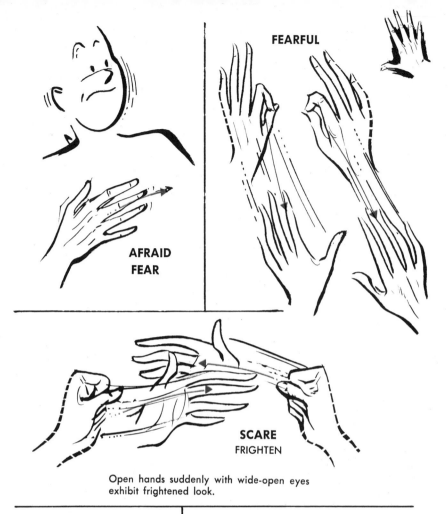

FEARFUL

**AFRAID
FEAR**

SCARE
FRIGHTEN

Open hands suddenly with wide-open eyes
exhibit frightened look.

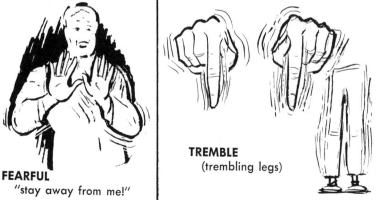

FEARFUL
"stay away from me!"

TREMBLE
(trembling legs)

387

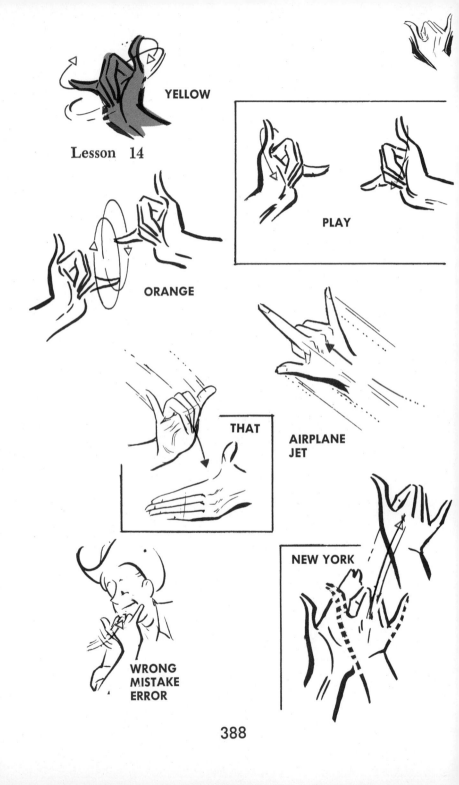

YELLOW

Lesson 14

PLAY

ORANGE

THAT

AIRPLANE
JET

WRONG
MISTAKE
ERROR

NEW YORK

388

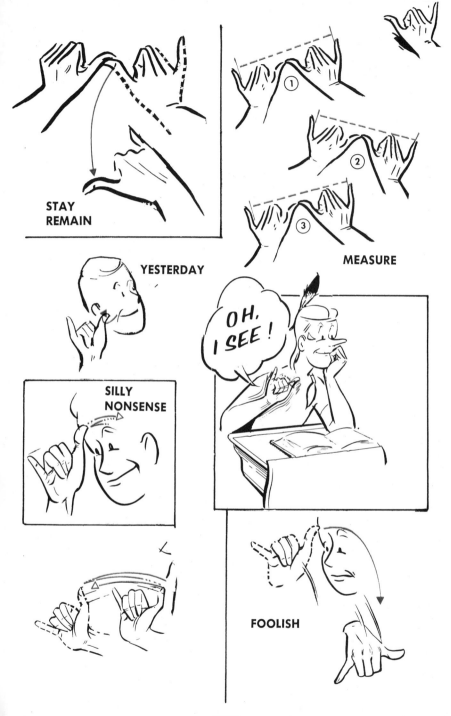

STAY
REMAIN

MEASURE

YESTERDAY

OH,
I SEE!

SILLY
NONSENSE

FOOLISH

389

SIGNS USED ON THE FACE OR AROUND THE HEAD

Lesson 15

SMILE

LAUGH

Stifling a laugh or emotion

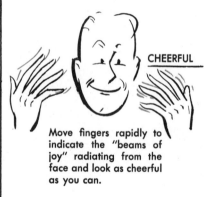

CHEERFUL

Move fingers rapidly to indicate the "beams of joy" radiating from the face and look as cheerful as you can.

"burst out laughing"

①

HYSTERICAL LAUGH

(Rolling all over the aisle)

②

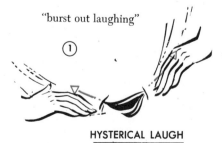

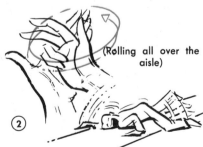

390

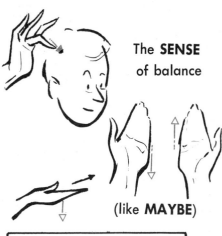

The **SENSE** of balance

(like **MAYBE**)

. . of sight

the **EAR**

"I HEAR" ✓

"I LISTEN"

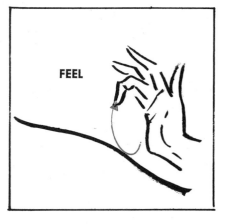

FEEL

. . of feel

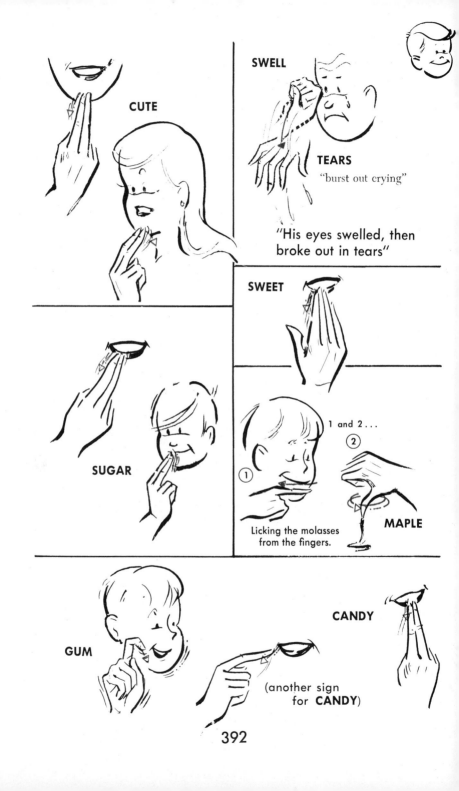

CUTE

SWELL

TEARS
"burst out crying"

"His eyes swelled, then broke out in tears"

SWEET

SUGAR

① ②
1 and 2 . . .

Licking the molasses from the fingers.

MAPLE

GUM

CANDY

(another sign for **CANDY**)

392

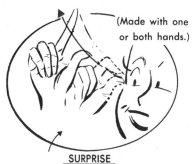

(Made with one or both hands.)

SURPRISE

Representing the motion of opening the eyes suddenly and look surprise.

AWAKE

- "come to" (from a fainting spell)
  "stay up"

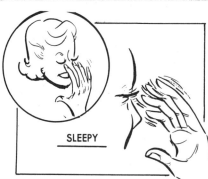

SLEEPY

WIDE AWAKE

- "stay up" (all night)

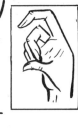

SLEEP

CRY

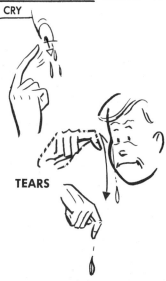

TEARS

"She **WINKED** at me!"

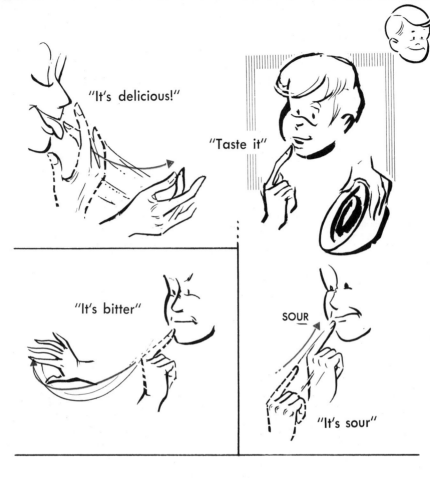

"It's delicious!"

"Taste it"

"It's bitter"

SOUR

"It's sour"

"SMELL it"

UGH!

ADORE

(the "A" over the heart)

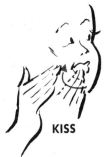

KISS

PET

MY FAVORITE

MY PET

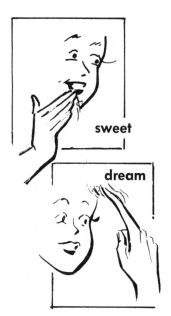

sweet

dream

Sweet dream . . and here's
a special kiss for
you!

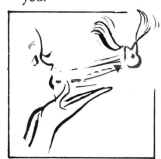

See page 408a

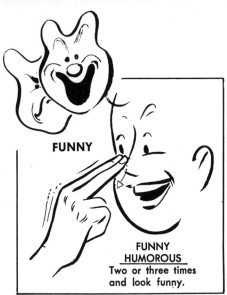

FUNNY

FUNNY
HUMOROUS
Two or three times
and look funny.

FUNNIEST + (thing)

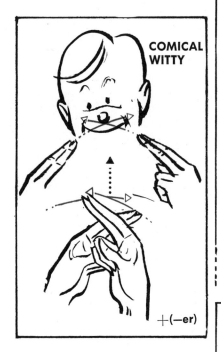

COMICAL
WITTY

+(−er)

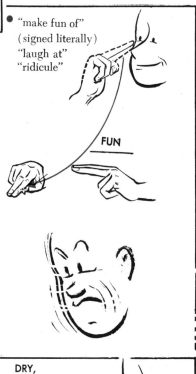

"make fun of"
(signed literally)
"laugh at"
"ridicule"

FUN

DRY,
DULL,
BORING

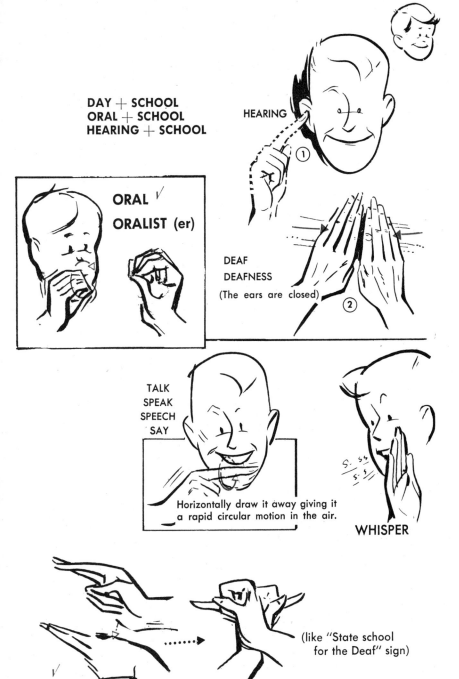

DAY + SCHOOL
ORAL + SCHOOL
HEARING + SCHOOL

HEARING

①

ORAL ✓

ORALIST (er)

DEAF
DEAFNESS
(The ears are closed)

②

TALK
SPEAK
SPEECH
SAY

Horizontally draw it away giving it
a rapid circular motion in the air.

WHISPER

(like "State school
for the Deaf" sign)

✓

RESIDENTIAL + SCHOOL

397

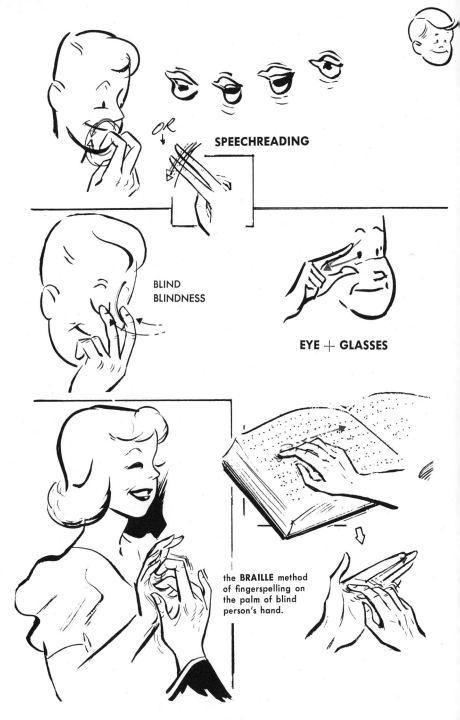

SPEECHREADING

BLIND
BLINDNESS

EYE + GLASSES

the **BRAILLE** method
of fingerspelling on
the palm of blind
person's hand.

398

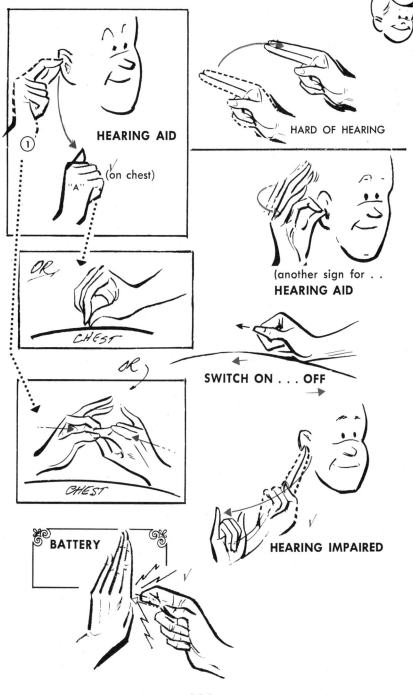

HEARING AID

"A" (on chest)

① OR (CHEST)

OR (CHEST)

BATTERY

HARD OF HEARING

(another sign for . .
HEARING AID

SWITCH ON . . . OFF

HEARING IMPAIRED

399

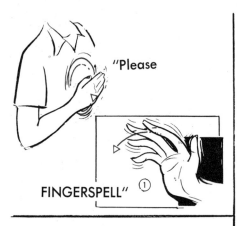

"Please

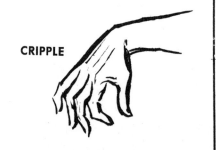

FINGERSPELL" ①

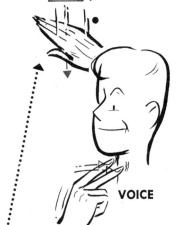

"Please <u>raise</u> your VOICE"

"Please <u>lower</u> your VOICE"

CRIPPLE

VOICE

> also used for . . .
> "Please raise the bed"
> "Please lower the bed"

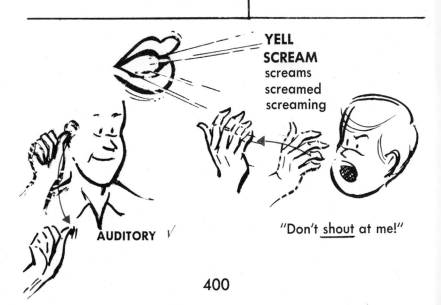

YELL
SCREAM
screams
screamed
screaming

AUDITORY √

"Don't <u>shout</u> at me!"

400

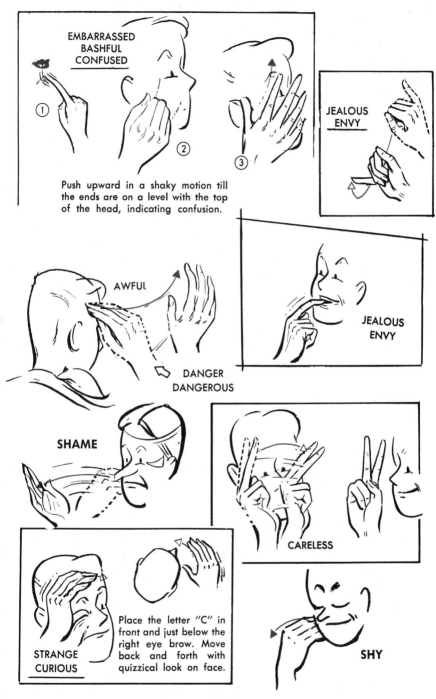

EMBARRASSED BASHFUL CONFUSED

① ② ③

Push upward in a shaky motion till the ends are on a level with the top of the head, indicating confusion.

JEALOUS ENVY

AWFUL

DANGER DANGEROUS

JEALOUS ENVY

SHAME

CARELESS

STRANGE CURIOUS

Place the letter "C" in front and just below the right eye brow. Move back and forth with quizzical look on face.

SHY

401

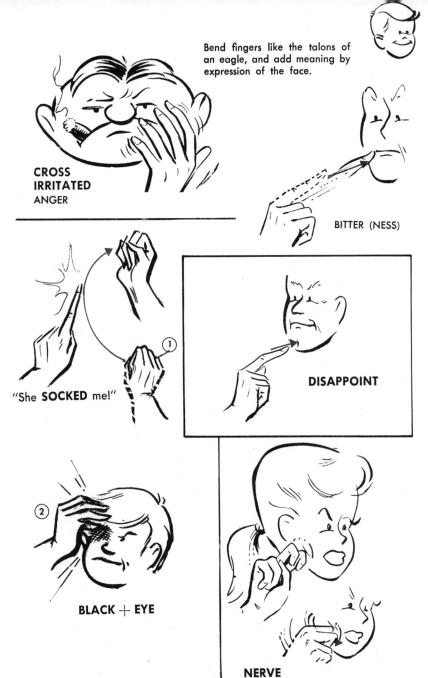

Bend fingers like the talons of an eagle, and add meaning by expression of the face.

CROSS
IRRITATED
ANGER

BITTER (NESS)

"She **SOCKED** me!"

DISAPPOINT

BLACK + EYE

NERVE
NERVY

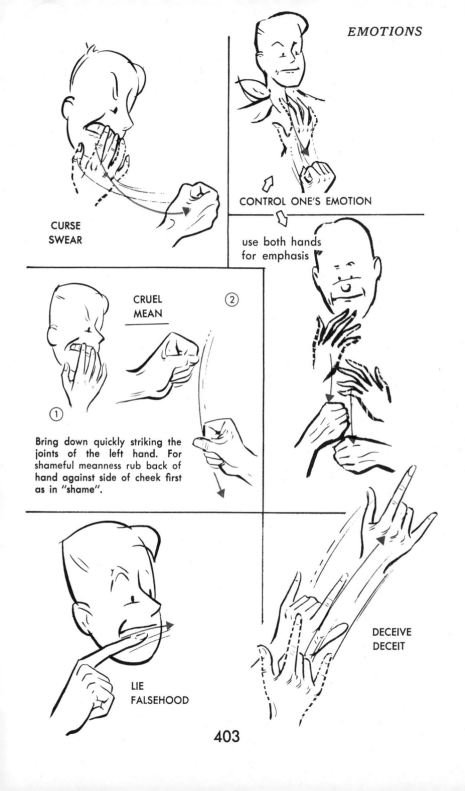

CURSE
SWEAR

CONTROL ONE'S EMOTION

use both hands
for emphasis

CRUEL
MEAN

②

①

Bring down quickly striking the
joints of the left hand. For
shameful meanness rub back of
hand against side of cheek first
as in "shame".

DECEIVE
DECEIT

LIE
FALSEHOOD

IGNORE or TO CUT

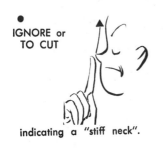

indicating a "stiff neck".

**PATIENCE
PATIENT**

Press on lips and bow head in resignation; repeat latter motion once or twice.

"can't take it anymore"
"put up with"   (patience + continue)
                (can't + bear)
                (can't + patience)

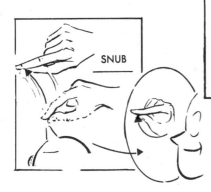

SNUB

**SILENCE
PATIENCE**

**TEDIOUS
MONOTONOUS**   ("The Grind".)

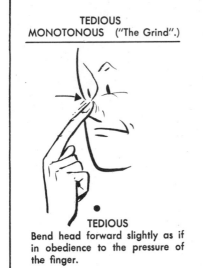

TEDIOUS
Bend head forward slightly as if in obedience to the pressure of the finger.

STUBBORN

mental +

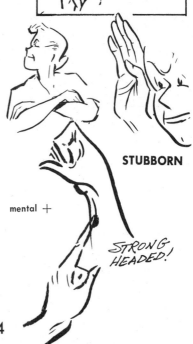

STRONG HEADED!

Lesson 16

EXCLAMATION
of feelings
shock,
anger,
etc.

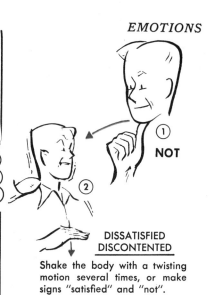

EMOTIONS

NOT

DISSATISFIED
DISCONTENTED

Shake the body with a twisting motion several times, or make signs "satisfied" and "not".

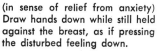

SATISFY
CONTENT
RELIEF

(in sense of relief from anxiety) Draw hands down while still held against the breast, as if pressing the disturbed feeling down.

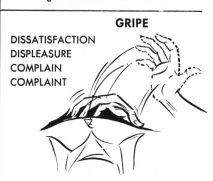

GRIPE

DISSATISFACTION
DISPLEASURE
COMPLAIN
COMPLAINT

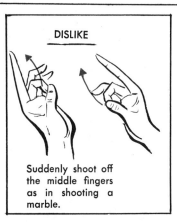

DISLIKE

Suddenly shoot off the middle fingers as in shooting a marble.

DISLIKE also made by sign for "LIKE" followed by "NOT".

405

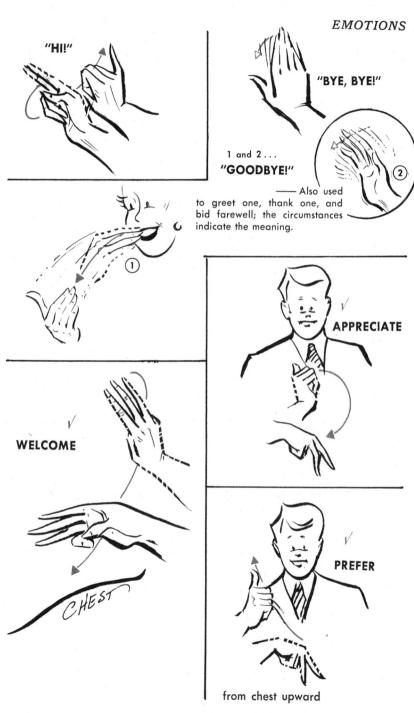

"HI!"

"BYE, BYE!"

1 and 2 . . .
"GOODBYE!"

—— Also used to greet one, thank one, and bid farewell; the circumstances indicate the meaning.

APPRECIATE

WELCOME

CHEST

PREFER

from chest upward

PLEASE

PLEASE
DELIGHTED

As if the heart is being drawn out toward the object. The sign for "please" is also used to mean "like."

LIKE
ENJOYMENT
PLEASE
PLEASURE
Rub over the heart with circular motion.

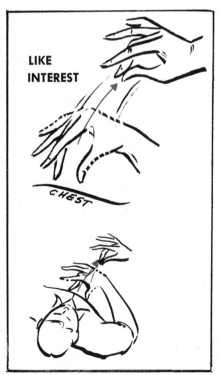

LIKE
INTEREST

CHEST

INTEREST (both hands)
FASCINATE

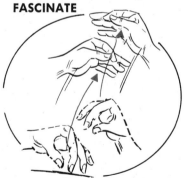

Draw away slowly from the heart giving the face an intent or concentrated look.

I LOVE YOU √
(the letter I-L-Y)

I LOVE YOU

I LOVE YOU, TOO

OR

DEAR √

DEAR (+ ly)

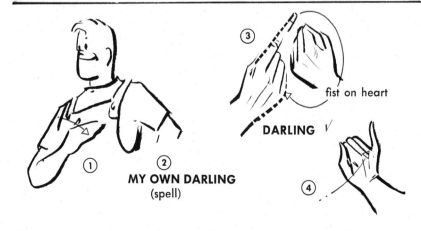

③ fist on heart

DARLING √

MY OWN DARLING
(spell)

① ② ④

408

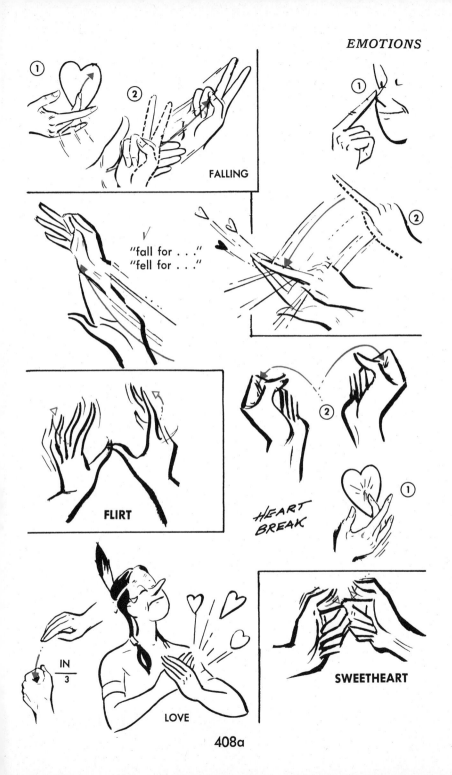

EMOTIONS

FALLING

"fall for . . ."
"fell for . . ."

FLIRT

HEART BREAK

LOVE

SWEETHEART

IN
3

408a

Circular motion over heart with appropriate expression.

SORROW
SORROWFUL

"I am sorry . . . .

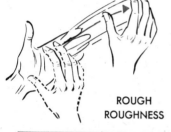

ROUGH
ROUGHNESS

SORRY

KIND
GENTLENESS

Move hands one around the other in a circle.

EXTREME ANGER
("MAD")

Give a tearing upward motion against the body. Sometimes both hands are used.

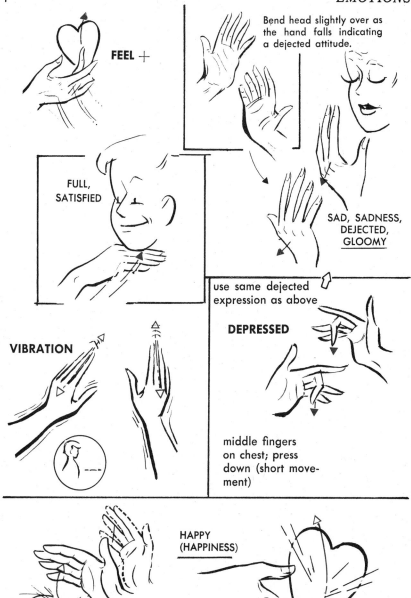

FEEL +

Bend head slightly over as the hand falls indicating a dejected attitude.

FULL, SATISFIED

SAD, SADNESS, DEJECTED, GLOOMY

use same dejected expression as above

DEPRESSED

VIBRATION

middle fingers on chest; press down (short movement)

HAPPY (HAPPINESS)

GLAD

Pat the heart with an upward motion repeated two or three times.

410

Avert face as if pushing off some unpleasant object.

**HATE
REPULSIVE**

DUMBFOUNDED
AT A LOSS
CONFUSED

Lower them with a jerk, bringing the body and hands somewhat rigid.

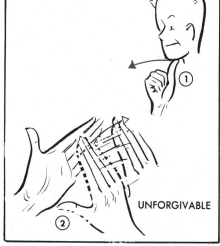

UNFORGIVABLE

HATE

CONSCIENCE

THUMP!

THUMP!

GIVE UP
LOSE HOPE
DISCOURAGED

Simultaneously with the action draw the head and shoulders back somewhat.

411

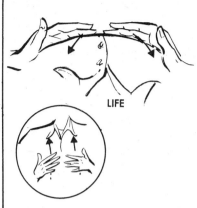

LIFE

LIFE
LIVE

ADDRESS
RESIDENCE

INSPIRE

EXCITEMENT
EXCITE

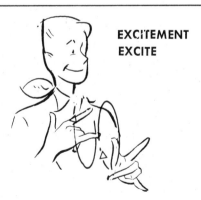

Draw first one then the other upward against the body and repeat, moving the hands alternately, assuming a nervous manner.

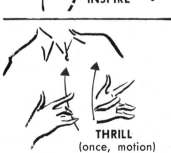

THRILL
(once, motion)

412

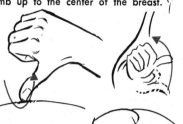

PRIDE

Throw chest out <u>proud</u>ly and draw the thumb up to the center of the breast.

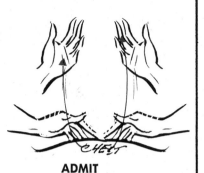

ADMIT
CONFESSION
also used for
VOMIT

BRAG (GING)
BOAST (ING)

BRAVE
COURAGE

● "take on"
"It would be nice if more employers 'take on' (hire) deaf employees"

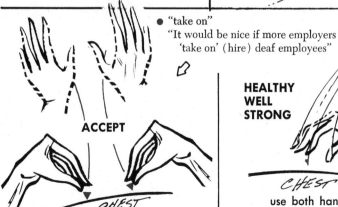

ACCEPT

HEALTHY
WELL
STRONG

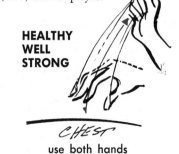

use both hands

413

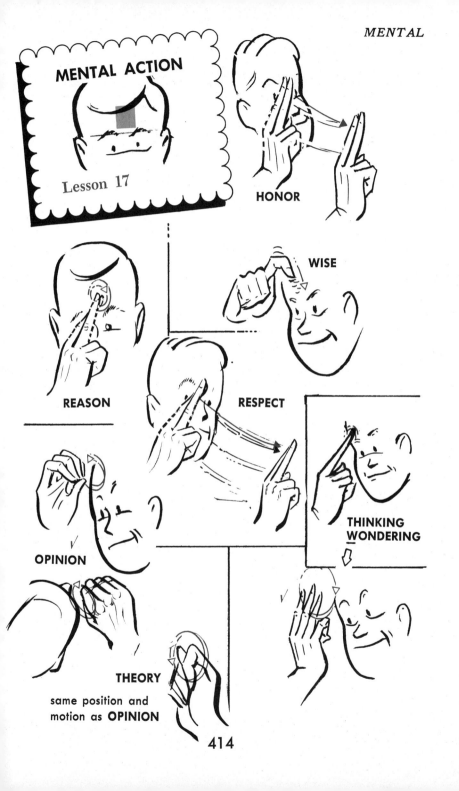

MENTAL ACTION

Lesson 17

HONOR

WISE

REASON

RESPECT

THINKING
WONDERING

OPINION

THEORY

same position and
motion as **OPINION**

414

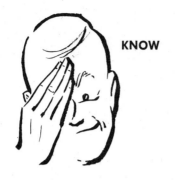

KNOW

THINK

"I think so."

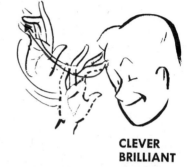

**CLEVER
BRILLIANT**

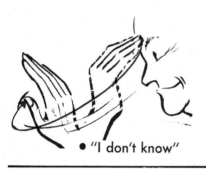

● "I don't know"

● "I knew it all the time"
(+ SINCE)

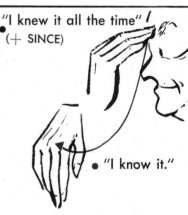

● "Don't you know?"
"Didn't you know?"

● "I know it."

"THINK!"

● "Use your head!" (brain)

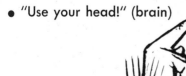

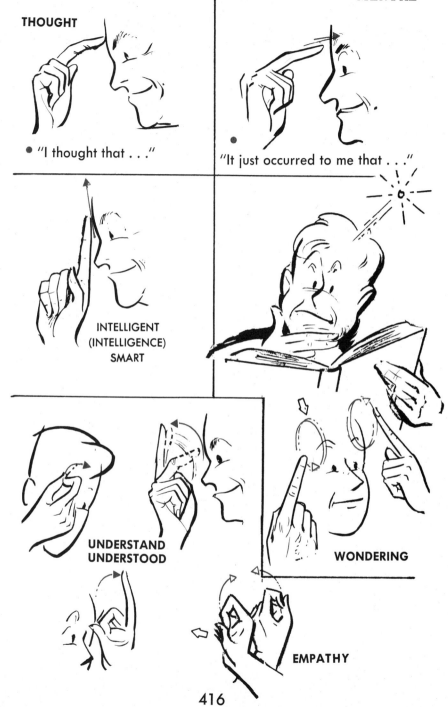

THOUGHT

• "I thought that . . ."

"It just occurred to me that . . ."

INTELLIGENT
(INTELLIGENCE)
SMART

UNDERSTAND
UNDERSTOOD

WONDERING

EMPATHY

416

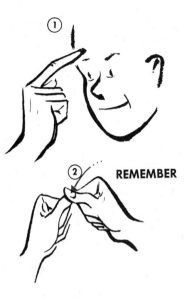

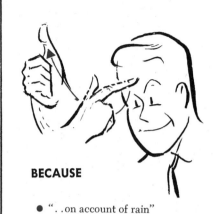

REMEMBER

BECAUSE

- ". . on account of rain"

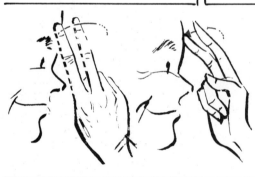

**MISUNDERSTAND
MISUNDERSTOOD**

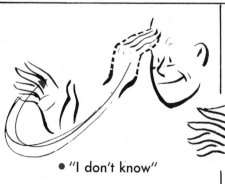

- "I don't know"

- "I don't care!"

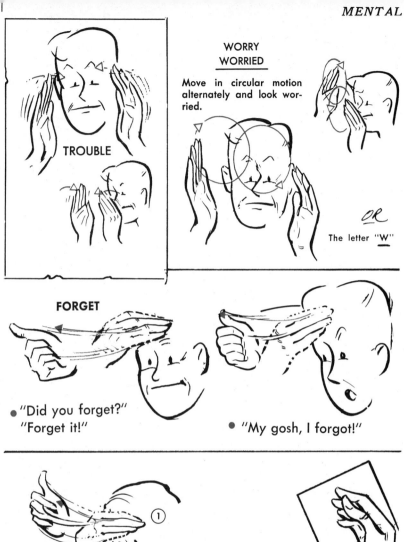

TROUBLE

WORRY
WORRIED

Move in circular motion alternately and look worried.

OR

The letter "W"

FORGET

● "Did you forget?"
 "Forget it!"

 ● "My gosh, I forgot!"

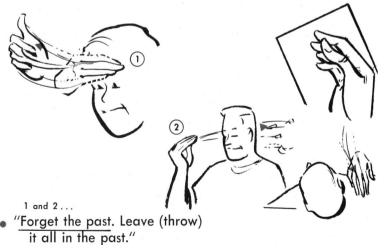

① ②

1 and 2 . . .
● "Forget the past. Leave (throw) it all in the past."

MIND
MENTAL
BRAINY

DREAM (+ er)

INVENT (+ or)

"I got an idea"
"What do you think
of my idea, (opinion)?"

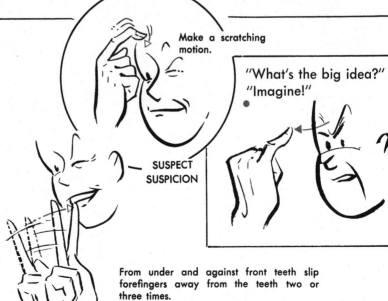

Make a scratching
motion.

"What's the big idea?"
"Imagine!"

SUSPECT
SUSPICION

From under and against front teeth slip
forefingers away from the teeth two or
three times.

419

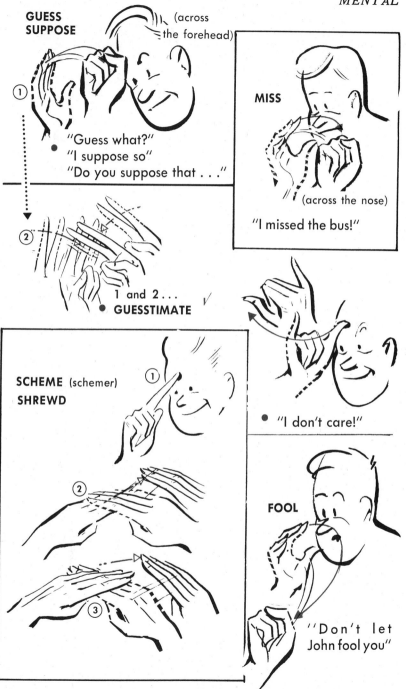

**GUESS
SUPPOSE**
(across the forehead)

① "Guess what?"
"I suppose so"
"Do you suppose that . . ."

MISS
(across the nose)
"I missed the bus!"

② 1 and 2 . . .
GUESSTIMATE

"I don't care!"

SCHEME (schemer)
SHREWD
①
②
③

FOOL
"Don't let
John fool you"

420

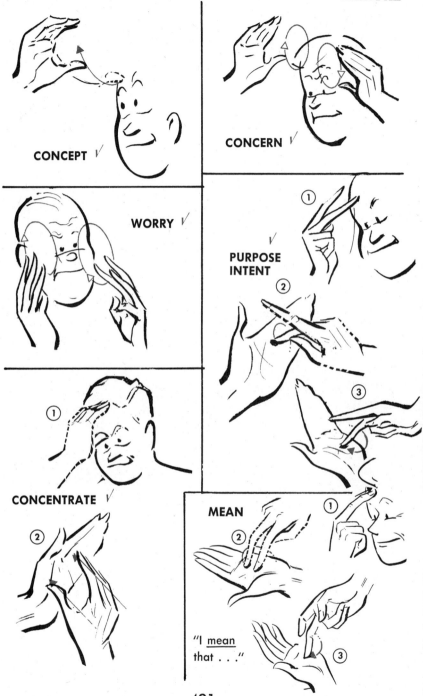

CONCEPT ✓

CONCERN ✓

WORRY ✓

PURPOSE INTENT ✓

① ② ③

CONCENTRATE ✓

① ②

MEAN

② ①

"I <u>mean</u> that . . ."

③

421

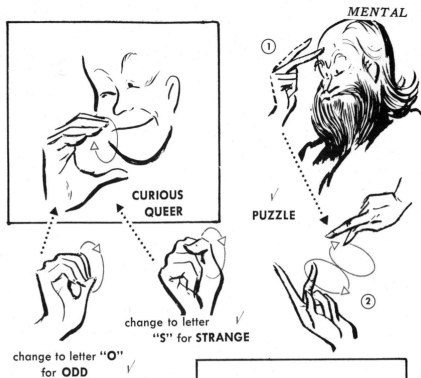

MENTAL

CURIOUS
QUEER

PUZZLE

change to letter
"S" for **STRANGE**

change to letter **"O"**
for **ODD**

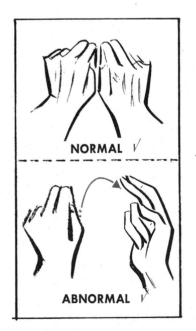

NORMAL

ABNORMAL

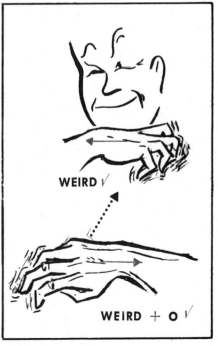

WEIRD

WEIRD + O

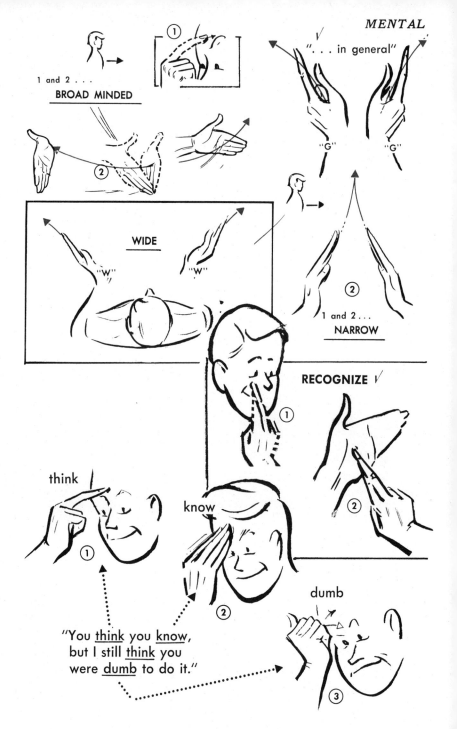

MENTAL

1 and 2 . . .
BROAD MINDED

". . . in general"

"G"   "G"

WIDE

"W"   "W"

1 and 2 . . .
NARROW

RECOGNIZE √

think

know

dumb

"You think you know,
but I still think you
were dumb to do it."

423

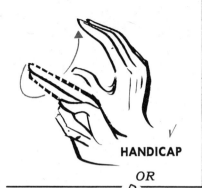

HANDICAP √

OR

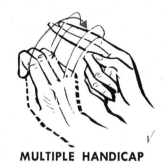

MULTIPLE HANDICAP √

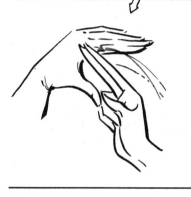

MENTAL RETARDED √

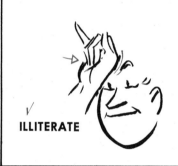

√ **ILLITERATE**

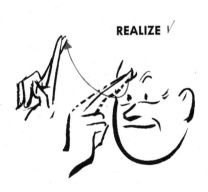

REALIZE √

424

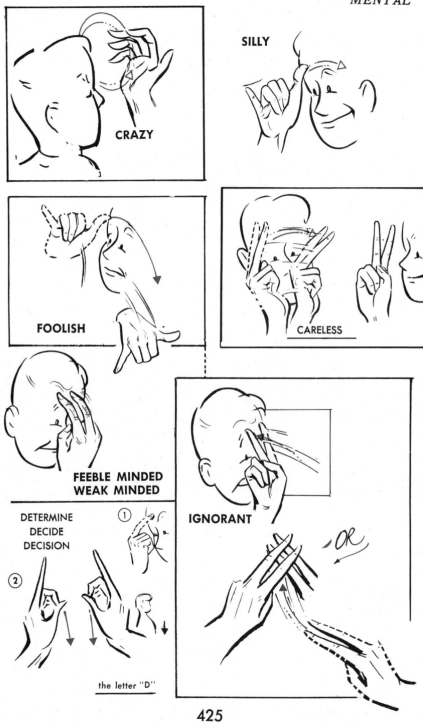

SILLY

CRAZY

FOOLISH

CARELESS

FEEBLE MINDED
WEAK MINDED

IGNORANT

DETERMINE
DECIDE
DECISION

① ②

OR

the letter "D"

425

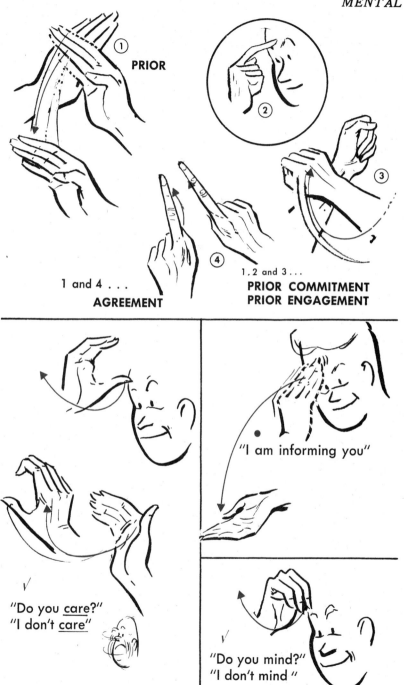

PRIOR

1 and 4 . . .
AGREEMENT

1, 2 and 3 . . .
PRIOR COMMITMENT
PRIOR ENGAGEMENT

"I am informing you"

"Do you <u>care</u>?"
"I don't <u>care</u>"

"Do you mind?"
"I don't mind"

426

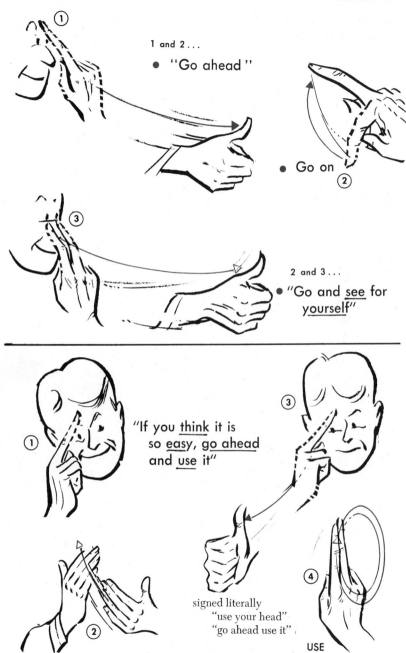

1 and 2...
● "Go ahead"

● Go on

2 and 3...
● "Go and <u>see</u> for <u>yourself</u>"

"If you <u>think</u> it is so <u>easy</u>, <u>go ahead</u> and <u>use</u> it"

signed literally
"use your head"
"go ahead use it"

USE

427

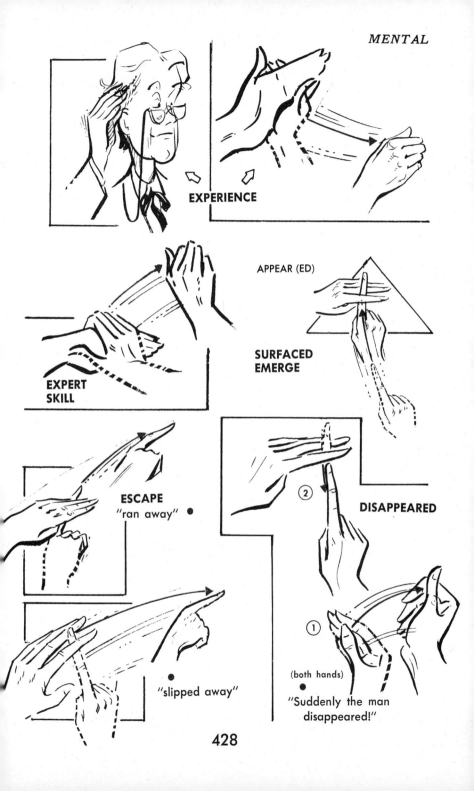

EXPERIENCE

EXPERT
SKILL

APPEAR (ED)

SURFACED
EMERGE

ESCAPE
"ran away" ●

DISAPPEARED

②

①

"slipped away"

(both hands)
●
"Suddenly the man
disappeared!"

428

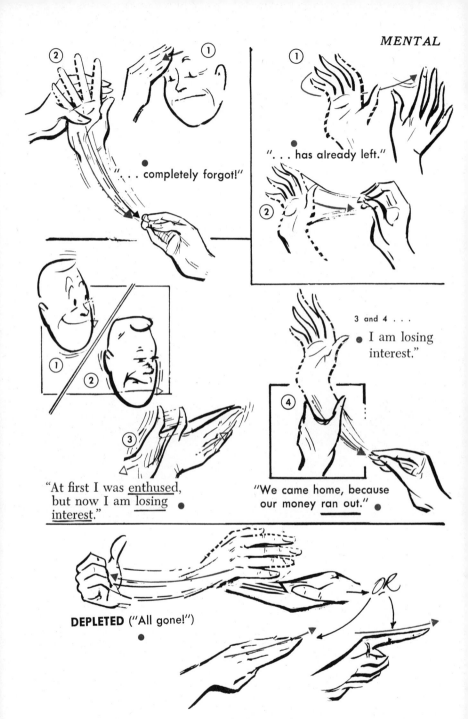

"... completely forgot!"

"... has already left."

3 and 4 ...
I am losing interest."

"At first I was <u>enthused</u>, but now I am <u>losing interest</u>."

"We came home, because our money ran out."

DEPLETED ("All gone!")

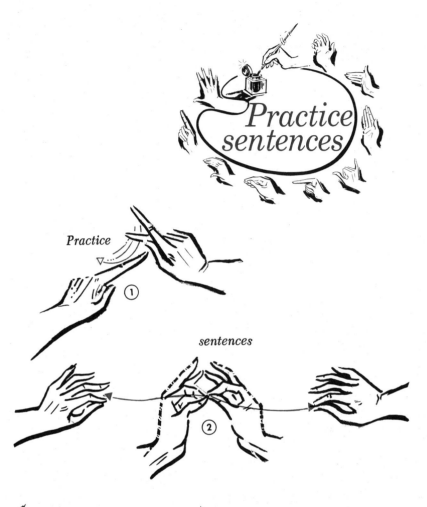

Practice sentences

Practice

①

sentences

②

See page 33-44c for additional practice sentences using the new verb forms designed for Signed English usage.

LESSON

Ⓐ

Practice Sentences

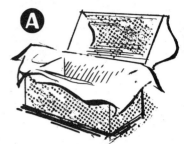

1. *Can* you *tell me* where the *red apple* is?

2. Is the apple *on the table* or in your *hand?*

3. No, it is *under* the table. It rolled and *fell* on *the floor.*

4. The apple *continued* to roll and *stopped between* the table and *chair.*

5. Is the apple *near* the chair or *far from it?*

6. No, it's right in the *center* between the chair and table.

7. Then what *happened?*

8. John picked it up and threw it to me.

9. I caught it and *set it* on the table.

10. Is the apple *inside* or *outside* your *lunch box* now?

11. It is *in front* of the box.

12. The lunch box is *behind* the apple.

13. That was very good. You may *go ahead* and *eat* your apple.

14. What? you said the apple is for *me?*

15. Oh, you *brought* this big, *shiny,* red apple just for me?

16. Oh, *that's very sweet and thoughtful of you!*

17. *Wait!* Don't bite on it yet. *Let me wash* and *polish it* for you.

I know.
I knew it.
I don't know. Why ask me?
Does anyone know the reason why?
I thought you knew.
I believe you should study more.
What were you thinking about?
A penny for your thoughts.
I often wondered why.
Wondered about what?
Why Dick is so suspicious.
We all think he is a wise man.
I agree (disagree) with you.
Did you understand what he said?
I don't know, and I don't care.
I may have misunderstood him.
There is no doubt about that.
What is John whispering about now?
Is he whispering about me?
I am curious to know what he said.
It isn't proper to whisper in front of me.
You are just imagining things.
Did you forget something?
No, I remembered to bring the money.
You're smart.

Did you understand what I said?
Yes, I think so.
Are you sure?
I don't know.
I may have misunderstood you.
All right. Let's start all over again.

"I have a large family.
I have three sisters and
three brothers."
"I have an Indian boy friend
and a girl friend."
"These are my six sisters.
I have six baby sitters."
"We have a small family. .
just two sisters."
"Whoopie! I have two dogs
and no sisters!"
"Meet my sister and two
brothers. We have fun
together."
"Meet my wife."
". .and this is my
husband."
"Have you met my
mother and father?
. .my parents?"
"We are their gra̶ndchildren."
"These are our children. It
is a large family."
"We also have many relatives.
Some of them live far away."
"That's our dad and mommy."
"Here are our gra̶ndparents!
We have lots of fun together!!"
"I miss you."

"Who is that sweet, little
lady walking out of the
office?"
"I wonder what that gentleman
is looking at?"

. .second CHILDHOOD

433

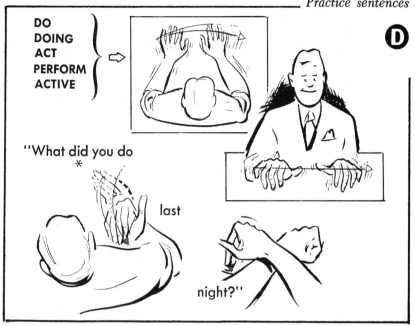

DO
DOING
ACT
PERFORM
ACTIVE

D

"What did you do
*

last

night?"

1. Must I do it now?
2. Yes, do it now . . . not tomorrow, nor the next day!
3. I told you what to do and why.
4. Look at Jim. He did it all by himself.

5. What are you going to do Sunday?
   Wednesday evening?
   Thursday noon?
   Friday night?
   all day (all night) Saturday?
   today?
6. What do you intend to do in Chicago?
7. Please act your age.
   *
8. Behave yourself!
9. John is very active for his age.
10. Mary acted as though she knew everything.
11. His performance was incomparable . . . it was super!
12. He showed us how to do it. It wasn't simple.
13. Do you think he will perform for us again?
   *

434

FAMILY—RELIGION—FOOD

1. I want you to meet my aunt and *uncle who are visiting* us this *week*.

2. *All my cousins live outside* of Chicago.

3. We *always thought* my brother would *remain a bachelor*.

4. All our *relatives* and *close friends came* to the wedding.

5. My *family goes to Bible study class in church* Wednesday evening.

6. Your *sister-in-law looked* for you in church this *morning*.

7. *Religion* and any type of *worship* is not permitted in the public *schools*.

8. Were you *baptized* in the *Catholic* or Lutheran church?

9. *Mother* went *shopping for groceries* for the *entire week*.

10. That *smells delicious, what's cooking?*

11. *Frozen food takes longer* to cook *than fresh food.*

12. Please *don't pour any gravy on my meat.*

13. *A long time ago, milk came with cream* on the top of every bottle.

14. What would you like to *drink,* I'm *thirsty,* too.

15. You have a *choice* of coffee, tea, milk or pop.

16. *Most children* are *satisfied* with *peanut butter* and *jelly sandwiches.*

17. Did your husband stop *smoking* those *awful cigars?*

18. You *must* be 21 *before* they will *serve* you *beer* or *whiskey.*

19. *Many* of the children *got sick* from *eating* those green *sour apples.*

20. Ice *cold watermelon tastes* good on a *hot day.*

21. *Pumpkin pie* is *always* a good *ending* for *Thanksgiving dinner.*

22. You *put* too *much salt and pepper* on the *potatoes.*

23. His *glory* is in the *heavens* and the *earth.*

24. You must *resist* the *temptation* to *lie and cheat.*

SIGNS used IN
and AROUND the House

1. I was *sleepy* this morning and didn't want to *get up*.

2. The *little girl* was *afraid* to *sleep* in the *dark alone*.

3. Please *wash* the *windows before* you put up the screens.

4. If you *lie down* for a *half hour, maybe* you will *feel better*.

5. Mother *washed clothes* Saturday *morning* and hung them *outside* to dry.

6. If you *take a cold shower* in the morning, *it will wake* you up.

7. The gardener *could not* find *his pick and shovel*.

8. The *flowers* are all in *bloom* and the *yard* looks *beautiful*.

9. *Remember* to *use the new forks, knives and* spoons for our *Sunday* dinner.

10. The children were up *all night—talking and giggling* and the *noise* kept us *awake*.

11. *When school is out,* I will *look for a part time* job.

12. *Ask* your *doctor* if you can *change* your *appointment* to a *later time.*

13. When you finish the test, *bring you paper* to me and *leave the room.*

14. We *expect* to *get* the results of the tests *next week.*

15. We *discovered* that the T.V. was *not working because* it was not *plugged* in.

16. *Every morning,* it is a good habit to wash your hands and face and brush your teeth.

17. *Don't forget* to get a *haircut* tomorrow.

18. My *uncle* had a *heart attack* and was rushed to the *hospital.*

19. I *hate* to go to the *dentist* to have my teeth *examined.*

20. He *fell* and cut his knee. I was *bleeding badly.*

21. Her *husband* had a *mental breakdown* and had to *rest* for 6 weeks.

NEED
MUST
HAVE TO
SHOULD
OUGHT TO
NECESSARY
} *Page 126*

"Do you <u>need</u> it?"
"Yes, I need it."
"I think you <u>should</u>
    go now."
"Do you think I <u>ought</u>
    to see my doctor?"
"You <u>must</u> do it now,
    before it's late."
"You don't <u>have to</u>
    do that."
"That isn't <u>necessary</u>."
"It won't be necessary."

"I <u>have to</u> go over . . .

"I <u>should</u> go over. . .

"I <u>ought</u> to go over . . .

"<u>Must</u> you go over now?"

            and pick up the car"

                see how Joe is."

                tell Mary about it."

Page 76-89

The ball is entering the..
　　　is rolling into..
　　　is rolling out of..
　　　is inside the..
　　　is hanging above the..
　　　is in front of..
　　　is behind the..
　　　is in back of..
　　　is on top of..
　　　rolled off the top
　　　is near the..
　　　is far from the..

Page 12-13

"..take a few."

"..take several"

"..take as many as
　you wish"

"Hold on! I didn't say
　you could take **ALL** of it."

"Is that all?"

"It doesn't matter. Take
　the first or second cookie."

Page 109-117

"Turn on the switch"
"Pull the button"
"Push the button in"
"Hang your coat"
"Turn on the light"
"Dim the light"
"Ring the doorbell"
"Knock on the door"
"Pound on the door"
"Shake the post"
"Wash the dishes"
"Wash the clothes"
"Iron the clothes"
"Sew the dress"
"Wash the windows"
"Scrub the floor"

　"Stand up!"
"Get in"　"Climb in"
"Get off"　"Let me off"
"Go!"
"I hear that . . ."
"Tell him"
"I see that . . ."

General

"It fits"
"I get a kick out
　of you"
"They were invited
　to our party"
"I hope they'll
　invite me"
"You have a right to . . ."
". . . . nosing the bait"
"I wrote her"
"She wrote me back"
"We still write to each other"
"We write back and forth"
"Store it in there"
"Put it on the shelf"
"Place it up higher,
so the kids can't reach it"
"John gulped it all"
"The teacher gave the
students some good advice"
"She also gave me
　some advice."
"I was left all alone"
"I'll be done in a second"

O

"... later on"
"... in the future"
"... far in the future"
"... a week ago"
"... last week"
"... two weeks ago"
"... three weeks ago"
"... two weeks from now"
"... three weeks from now"
"... just a little while ago"
"... a short time ago"
"... just recently"

".. the other day"
".. a few days ago"
".. every so often"
".. now and then"
".. up till now"
".. all along since"
"seldom"
"occasionally"
"once in a great while"
".. way back before.."
".. long before that"
".. back in '41, '42, '43, etc."

{
.. somewhere between 50 and 60
.. In the neighborhood of 30-40

.. costs around $5 ... $8.00

.. drove between 55 and 65 miles an hour.

J

"He looks familiar"
"He is one of our ancestors"
"How many children do
        you have left?"
"All of our children are grown"
"Finally, we have raised our children"
"John resembles his father"
"She takes after her mother
                    father
                    sister
                    daughter
                    son

"You haven't changed a bit!"
"Both girls look exactly alike"
"John looks just like
        his Uncle"
"..still very young"
"..middle aged"

Page 343-344

"John came alone"
"He went alone"
"She came and met me."
"He walked toward me"
"We ran into each other"
"I went up to him"
"All alone"
"We finally made it over
 the mountains"
"only a dollar"

General

"Come and join us"
"Cross it out"
"From now on.."
"I pity you"
"instead of.."
"put off..put off, etc."
"John appears to
 avoid us"
"Helen saw me, but
 walked away."

Page 141

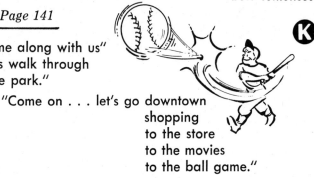

"Come along with us"
"Let's walk through
    the park."
    "Come on . . . let's go downtown
                        shopping
                        to the store
                        to the movies
                        to the ball game."

Page 128-140

"How much is it?"
"What's the total charge?"
"Are there any left?"
"This one is for only
    a dollar!"

". . . a dime"   ". . . fifty cents"
". . . ten cents"   ". . . a half dollar"
". . . five cents"   ". . . twenty cents"
". . . a nickel"   ". . . thirty cents"
". . . twenty five cents" ". . . forty cents"
". . . a quarter"

                        "Here's a dime for you, you
                            and you."

Page 131-139

"None left"
"Nothing left (remains)"
"The office offered to
    pay for my meals"
"I offered to pay
    for our dinner"

Page 414-247

L

"Didn't you know?"
"I know it."
"I knew it all the time" (+ SINCE)
"I got an idea"
"What do you think
   of my idea, (opinion)?"
"What's the big idea?"
"Imagine!"

"It just occurred to me that . . ."
"I thought that . . ."
"I think so."
"It made me think . . ."
"I wonder?"

Page 420

"Guess what?"
"I suppose so"
"Do you suppose that . . ."
"I missed the bus!"
   Don't let
   John fool you"

Page 170-177

Page 91-108

"Take your hat off"
"Take your coat off"
      shoes
      glasses

"Go upstairs and
   comb your hair"

"Don't litter the yard."

"Go and pick them up,
and throw them in the
trash basket"

"Please pour some cream
   in my oatmeal."
"A little more"
"Still more"
"Just a bit more"
"Add some more"
"That's enough!"
"FINISH!"
"STOP!!"
"Wow! That's a little
   too much!"
"Sorry. I wasn't looking"
      "I wasn't thinking"
"You didn't use
   your judgment!"

438f

Page 118-125

"SURPRISE!"

"I am surprised to
see you here!"

"Come on in."

"Come on . . . let's go
now before the store is
closed. Perhaps we are
late."

"Hungry? Let's go eat"

"Must you go now?"

"We're going later."
            in a little while."

"Why are you going
so early?"

"I came all the way here,
and all the way back
. . . for nothing!"

"Don't hold her . . . let her go!"

"Take her with you"

"get ahead"

"falling behind"

"catching up"

"slipped back"

". . in back of the door"

". . stand in back of me"

". . far out in front"

". . way ahead of the field"

". . the dog ran after the car"

"The boy stood alongside
of the car"

Page 467-468

"Did you know that . . ."
"Have you heard about . . ."
"Did you hear about . . ."
"Someone told me that . . ."
"It's being rumored that . . ."
"He said that . . .

      John was hit by a trolley
      and was rushed to the
      hospital"

      . . . became very ill (sick)"

General

"Look like . ."
(face + same)
"Look for . ."
"Look at . . ."
"Look to . ."

438g

Keep your closet clean and neat.
Always hang your clothes and
   keep everything in order.
Who borrowed my toothpaste,
   my boots, socks?
I thought I saw someone set it there.
I pulled out all the drawers and
   rummaged through them.
Whose sock is this?
Where did you find it?
I found it way underneath the pile.
Which dress should I wear this evening?
One of my dresses is too small.
Why don't you take it back
   and exchange it?
I had better go in and change
   the bed sheets and pillows.
Would you like a clean, fresh pillow?
Good night . . . I am going to bed.
I think I'll hop in bed.

Page 118-125

"John will be back in
a few minutes."
a little while."

"We will have to go
there again."

"Go in again and see."

"Send it back."
"Return your dress
for a larger size."

"Come back again."

"They came again, again,
and again!"

Page 63-69

"Is that the one?"
"Are those the ones?"
"The girls don't look alike"
"Each girl varies in size
  and shape"
"It's hard to tell them apart."
"How can you tell one
   from the other?"

"Have you taken the pill?"
"I was forced to . . ."

PREPARING for the TRIP

1. Are you done packing?

2. Yes, I am *almost finished. I hope* I haven't *forgotten* anything.

3. How many suitcases are you *taking along?*

4. One *good, large* size is all I *need.*

5. Have you *made* your *reservation?*

6. *The morning train/plane/bus has already left.* So I am taking the afternoon train.

7. Will you *come* to the station with me, and *see me* off?

8. Oh, I would be *delighted* to *accompany you.*

9. *Here we are.* It *didn't take long.*
   Will you *please* interpret for me?

10. *Ask* the agent how long it will take to *reach* Chicago.

11. He said it takes three hours and 37 minutes.

12. *That's almost* four hours!

13. *Imagine! Last year* it took me only three hours and nine minutes to fly by jet to *California.*

14. *Anyway,* I think it will be *more fun* to ride the train, and not *worry about* flying *35,000 feet* above the ground.

15. Did you *get* the *ticket?* How much was the fare?

16. Well, by 6:15 this evening I shall be in Chicago.

17. You had *better hurry* now, or you will miss the train.

18. Goodbye . . . *enjoy yourself* and have a good time!

ILLNESS and MEDICINE

<u>In doctor's office</u> . . .

1. May *I see the doctor?*

2. You may *go in* now.

3. I don't *feel* well. I think I am *ill.*

4. I *have a headache, a stomach ache, a pain here.*

5. It *bothered me* for *several hours,* all night, for two days.

6. I have *chills* and my chest *hurts.*

7. I had been *coughing* for several days.

8. I have had a *hard* time breathing.

9. My arm, shoulder, head, back *hurts.*

10. I have had cramps. Sometimes I *feel* like *vomiting.*

11. Please *examine* this wound.

12. My arms are bruised and cut.

13. My eyes are blurred, I cannot see very well.

14. Why *didn't* you come sooner?

15. *Show me* where it hurts.

16. I'll examine you. Take off your shirt, clothes.

17. . . . open your mouth   . . . inhale

18. . . . stick out your tongue   . . . exhale
                                . . . hold your breath

19. You have a *temperature.* You have high blood pressure.

20. How long have you been ill?

21. Have you *taken* any *medicine?*

22. You need a *complete physical examination.*

23. I will *give you an injection,* and prescribe some medicine for you.

24. I will *call* your *druggist.* It'll be *ready* for you.

25. Take this in water three times a day.

26. Take a spoonful *before* you eat.

27. *Do not* eat *anything after 4 o'clock.*

28. Then take these two pills before going to *bed.*

LAW and TRAFFIC

1. That's the *courthouse.*

2. The *jail* is on the top floor of the courthouse.

3. *Prisoners* cannot *escape* from it.

4. It is for *criminals* or *lawbreakers.*

5. Lawbreakers must either pay *fine* or serve time in jail.

6. This town has a good *police force.*

7. They are our friends and *help* to protect us.

8. They also *control* the automobile traffic movements.

9. If you are *involved* in an accident, *call* the police.

10. Stop and see if anyone is injured.

11. If possible don't *move* the injured *body.*

12. *Ask* or *seek* for help immediately.

13. Give your *name and address,* then see your *lawyer.*

14. Do you know anyone who can be your interpreter?

15. You *should have* his name and *phone* number with you at all times.

16. See that your rear mirrors are clean and in position *before starting* a trip.

17. *Never* drive too close to another vehicle (car).

18. *Always keep* your eyes on the *road.* Be alert for other cars.

19. *Observe speed regulation.* (follow)

20. Yield right of *way.*

21. Be *courteous.*

22. Stop, look, listen.

Person to person conversation

For intermediate and advanced students
(Red dot • denotes 2nd person)

1. *Find* the *word* in the *dictionary.*
   - Here it is!
     It's on page 22 and it *spells* w-o-r-d.

2. I *wonder* where he *went.*
   - I haven't the *faintest idea.*
     Does *anyone else know?*

3. Do you *remember* your *promise?*
   - You *ought* to know *better.*
     I never *break* my promise.

4. *Show* me the *way* to go *home.*
   - How did you get *here* in the *first place?*

5. This *subject* is very *interesting.*
   - Which subject are you *talking about?*

6. The *English language* is *difficult* to *learn.*
   - The *more* you read, the *easier* it becomes.

7. I don't know how to sign that word.
   - You don't? I have shown you twice how to sign it.
     Please *concentrate* and *watch* me do it.

8. *That* is a good *idea.*
   - I am *sorry* but I *disagree* with you.

9. I *like arithmetic* and *history.*
   - *I don't care* for mathematics.
     But I *enjoy art, music,* and *poetry.*

10. He *announced* his *plans* for *college.*
    - I am not *surprised.* He is very *intelligent.*
      He will go *far* in *life.*

11. The lesson was *postponed* from last week.
    - That was *because* you were *absent* all *week.*
      Were you *sick?*

12. Can you *hear* that *beautiful music?*
    - Yes, I can hear it, but I *don't understand* the words.

13. The *cop warned* the boy about *taking dope.*
    - If the boy doesn't *stop now.*
      he will be in *real trouble.*

14. Which *candidate* did you *select?*
    - At first, I liked John. But I *changed* my
      mind and *selected Donny.*

Person to person conversation

1. We *practice* with a *mirror.*
   • Who will hold the mirror for you?

2. Please see me *before* you *leave.*
   • Did I do something *wrong?*

3. If I am *out, wait* for me.
   • How *long* will you be *gone?*

4. *Someone* told us that *story.*
   • I *don't believe* it.

5. *Give me another* chance.
   • OK. I'll give you *another* chance *until tomorrow noon.*

6. *Association* with the deaf *people* helps *improve* your *signs.*
   • And *also* to read and *understand* them *better.*

7. Did you bowl *above* or *below* your average?
   • I *always* bowl above *except* when I bowl *against* you.

8. How is your baby *today?*
   • *Wonderful!* She *spoke* her *first* word *last night.*

9. Where can I find *more cookies?*
   • *Grandpa* ate them all up last night.

10. *Each* of us can *learn* in his own *way.*
    • It's always *fun* to learn *something new.*

11. Go *through* that door.
    • Why *can't* I go through the *other* door?

12. *When* can we get *together?*
    • We can *meet again at* the *same place,* same *time, next Saturday.*

13. Where did you *buy* your new hat?
    • I *made* it *myself.* Do you *like* it?

14. Tell me about your *vacation.*
    • I had a *terrible* time, and you had *better believe me!!*

15. He came *from New York.*
    • Oh, I am *glad* you *told* me. I thought he was from L.A.

16. All are *present* except that new student.
    • Should I *go out* and *look* for him?

17. Is this *book yours?*
    • Let me see. Yes, it is mine. Where did you find it?

18. When will you *finish* your *work.*
    • *I don't know.* I haven't *started* working *yet.*

Person to person conversation

1. *What* do you *want* for *lunch (breakfast) (dinner) tomorrow?*
   * I would like a lettuce, *tomato,* and bacon *sandwich.*
     Whatever you *serve* will be *fine* with me.

2. Please may I have some more milk?
   * Mother is in the kitchen. She will bring you some.

3. Never mind. I *can't wait any longer.*
   * Don't be so *rude. Keep quiet* and wait.

4. That boy is *hot tempered.*
   * He will *grow out of that.*

5. Why did you *disobey* your *mother?*
   * I am sorry. I *didn't mean* to be rude.

6. *Some children* are *selfish* with their toys.
   * I *can't understand why. Maybe*
     when they *get older,* they will be more generous.

7. The boy does *not want* to go *home now.*
   * I think you had *better call* his mother.

8. You *should* have a *little* more *patience* with that child.
   - *Perhaps* you are *right.*

9. My *sister* was *surprised* to see us.
   - How *long* has it been *since* she saw you?

10. It was a *thrilling experience.*
    - Tell us all about it.

11. Can you tell us more about your *past* experience?
    - Really, there isn't much to say.

12. If you are *bored,* we will stop now.
    - *Thank goodness,* it is about time.

13. *Many men and women* are *vain* about their *appearance.*
    - What's wrong with that?
      Turkeys like to be vain, too.

14. Will you please look at me for a minute?
    - OK. What have you got to say for yourself?

15. His *supervisor noticed* his *enthusiasm* and rewarded him with a *promotion.*
    - I am sure his *friends* will be *happy* to hear about it.

Person to person conversation

1. If you *improve enough,* you can *proceed* to the next lesson.
   - It appears to be *difficult,* but I'll *try.*

2. *Look* for the word in the dictionary.
   - I *know* what the word *means.*
     but I *don't know* the *sign* for it.

3. His parents are *separated* and *will probably* get a *divorce.*
   - We *hope* they will see *their mistakes,* and be *together again.*

4. The old *man* was very *angry.*
   - I know it. I *broke* his favorite *pipe.*

5. *Follow* me *while* I sign the *poem.*
   - You *mean* I *should* repeat after you?

6. *Don't* get excited about that.
   - I must learn to *restrain* myself.

7. This *pie* is *delicious.*
   - What kind of pie is it?

8. Tell me the *secret.*
   - I can't *trust* you.

9. That is a *very funny story* you told me.
   - Then why didn't you *laugh?*

10. My *mother* is always *cheerful* and *smiling*.
    - *People* who know her, *love* her.

11. She *disagreed* with their idea.
    - Can you think of a better idea?

12. *Don't make fun* of that boy.
    - I am sorry. I didn't realize what I was saying. I *apologize*.

13. The boy scout was very *kind* to the little old lady.
    - Yes. The old lady thanked him.
      She told him: "*You picked* good parents."

14. Why did you *fight* with your *brother*?
    - I had *nothing* else to do.

15. What are you *waiting* for? *Hurry!*
    - *Stop* pushing me around!

16. My *sister* is very *proud* of her *son*.
    - Anybody would be proud of that boy!

17. If you are *guilty,* confess the truth.
    - All right. I *admit* I *took* the cookies. Am I *forgiven*?

18. If you are *guilty,* confess the truth.

Person to person conversation

1. It is very *important* for us to know *exactly* how it *happened.*
   - It is our *responsibility* to get *all* the facts.

2. Don't be *lazy* and *careless* about your *appearance.*
   - Thank you for telling me.

3. My *new* hat is *pink and white.*
   - Are you going to wear it on *Easter Sunday?*

4. This lesson is *easier* than the one we had *yesterday.*
   - I am *beginning* to *enjoy* the lesson.

5. This view *from the window* is *beautiful.* Mary said she could sit here and watch the scenery *all afternoon.*

6. Do you like a *hard* or *soft* mattress?
   - I prefer *medium.*

7. How do you *want* your steak? . . . , rare, *medium,* or well done?
   - It doesn't matter but I want it *tender!*

8. My boy *friend* is *tall, dark,* and handsome.
   - Yes, but I think he is very conceited, too.

9. I *wish* I *could exchange* this white coat for a darker coat.
   - Why don't you take it back and exchange it?

10. Be *brave,* don't be a *coward like* that man in the *movie.*
    - I will *try* and be brave.

11. *Stand firm,* for what you *believe* is right.
    - You can be sure to *depend* on me.

12. He was *confused* and could not *find* his *way* home.
    - *Tell him* to *stay* in my *house* for a while.

13. You *should* have some *goal* in *life* and work for it.
    - But I *don't know* where to begin.

14. *Ignorance* is no fault of yours.
    - Just the same (nevertheless) I can't *help feeling stupid* some of the time.

15. The *old lady* was *weak* and *thin* from lack of food.
    - We must do all we can to help her.

16. New *born babies* have blue eyes.
    - Really? I never knew that. I *always* thought they were *brown.*

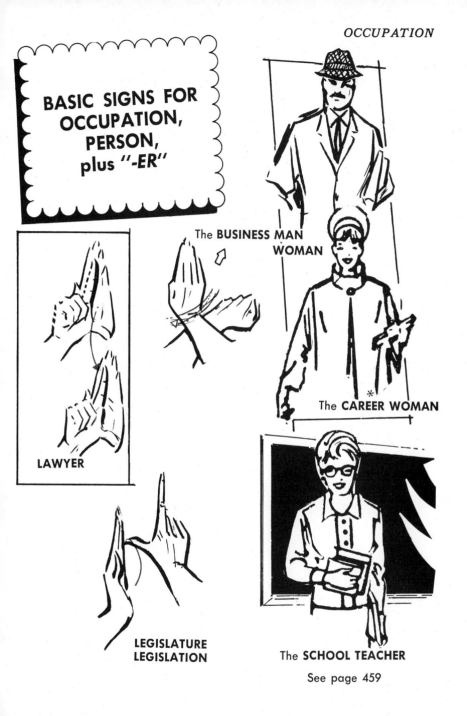

BASIC SIGNS FOR OCCUPATION, PERSON, plus "-ER"

The **BUSINESS MAN**
WOMAN

LAWYER

The **CAREER WOMAN**

LEGISLATURE
LEGISLATION

The **SCHOOL TEACHER**

See page 459

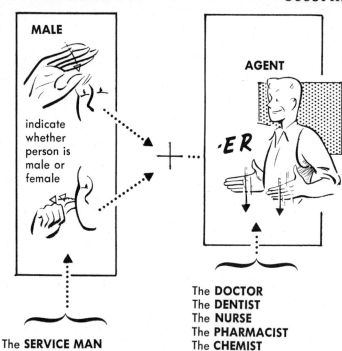

MALE

indicate whether person is male or female

AGENT

·ER

The **SERVICE MAN**
The **BUSINESS MAN**
The **SALESMAN**
The **"HARD HAT" MAN**
The **TELEPHONE MAN**
The **DELIVERY MAN**
The **REPAIR MAN**
The **MAIL MAN**
The **FIREMAN** fire + man
The **POLICE**
The **PATROLMAN**

The **DOCTOR**
The **DENTIST**
The **NURSE**
The **PHARMACIST**
The **CHEMIST**
The **SCIENTIST**
The **PRIEST**
The **MINISTER**
The **SCHOOL TEACHER**
The **CAREER WOMAN**
The **BANKER**
The **TAILOR**
The **CLEANER** clean + press
The **INDIAN**
The **COWBOY**
The **PILGRIM**
The **CARPENTER**
The **CABINET MAKER**
The **FARMER**
The **BAKER**
The **MECHANIC** auto + machine
The **WAITRESS**
The **WAITER**
The **TRUCK DRIVER**
The **ELECTRICIAN**
The **MAIL CARRIER**
The **SECRETARY**
The **COOK**
The **CHEF**
The **GROCERY CLERK**

AIDE

ASSISTANT

455

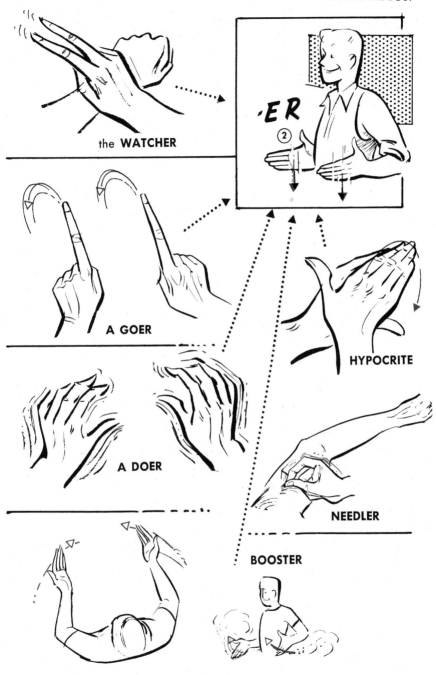

the **WATCHER**

A **GOER**

A **DOER**

HYPOCRITE

NEEDLER

BOOSTER

456

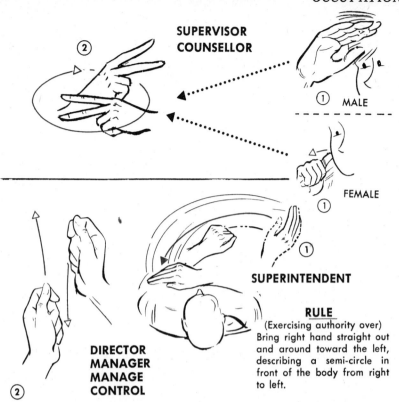

**SUPERVISOR
COUNSELLOR**

MALE

FEMALE

SUPERINTENDENT

**DIRECTOR
MANAGER
MANAGE
CONTROL**

RULE
(Exercising authority over)
Bring right hand straight out
and around toward the left,
describing a semi-circle in
front of the body from right
to left.

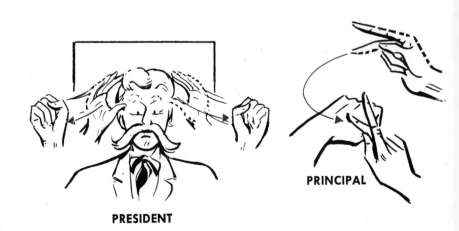

PRESIDENT

PRINCIPAL

457

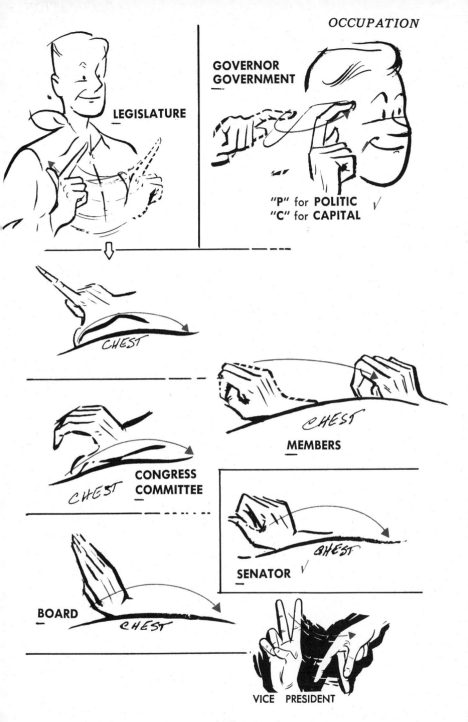

LEGISLATURE

GOVERNOR
GOVERNMENT

"P" for **POLITIC** ✓
"C" for **CAPITAL**

CHEST

MEMBERS
CHEST

CONGRESS
COMMITTEE
CHEST

SENATOR ✓
CHEST

BOARD
CHEST

VICE PRESIDENT

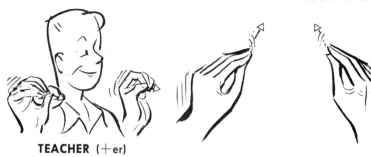

TEACHER (+er)

LEARNER
NOVICE
APPRENTICE } (+er)
PUPIL

INSTRUCT √
INSTRUCTION

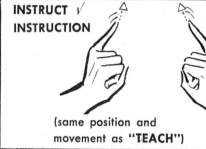

(same position and
movement as **"TEACH"**)

PROFESSOR √

ANALYZE

PHILOSOPHY √

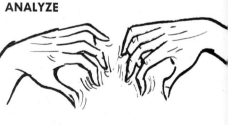

Sorting out . . .

459

PSYCHIATRIST
PSYCHIATRY

PSYCHOLOGY
PSYCHOLOGIST (+er)

The **SECRETARY**

BLACK (race)

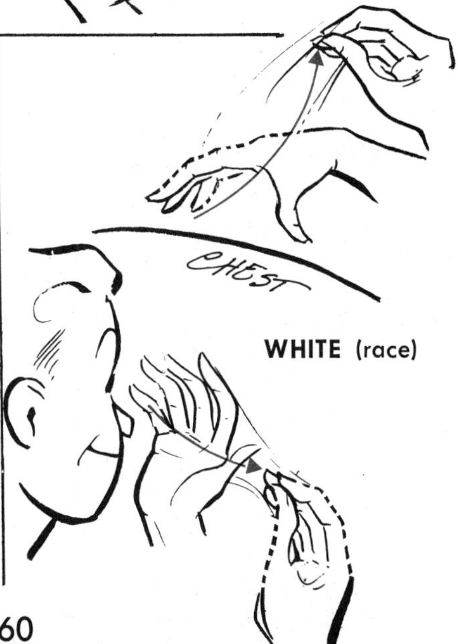

CHEST

WHITE (race)

460

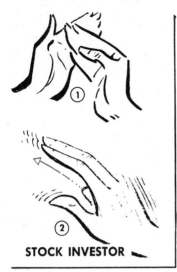

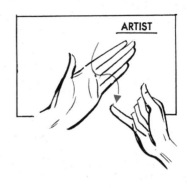

ARTIST

②

STOCK INVESTOR

SUBSCRIBE
SUBSCRIPTION

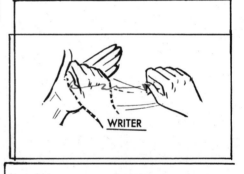

WRITER

The **BANKER
DEALER**

money +

SUBSTITUTE
EXCHANGE
TRADE

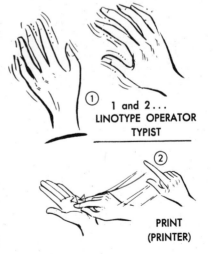

① 1 and 2 . . .
LINOTYPE OPERATOR
TYPIST

②

PRINT
(PRINTER)

461

WORK

WORK (ING)

JOB √

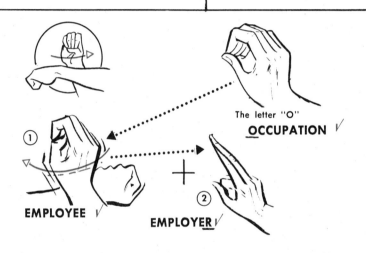

The letter "O"
OCCUPATION √

EMPLOYEE √

EMPLOYER √

① ②

+

LABOR √

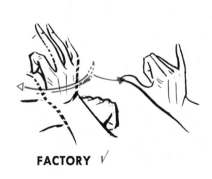

FACTORY √

462

PAINTER

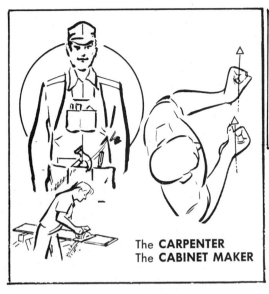

The **CARPENTER**
The **CABINET MAKER**

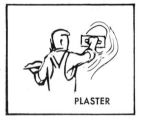

PLASTER

a pair of **PLIERS**

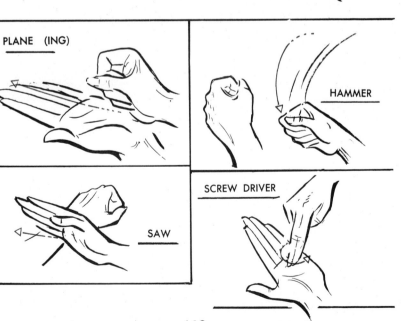

PLANE (ING)

HAMMER

SAW

SCREW DRIVER

463

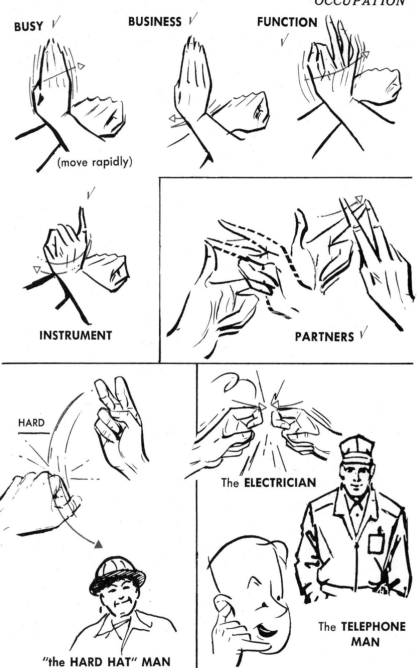

BUSY ✓

(move rapidly)

BUSINESS ✓

FUNCTION ✓

INSTRUMENT

PARTNERS ✓

HARD

"the HARD HAT" MAN

The ELECTRICIAN

The TELEPHONE MAN

464

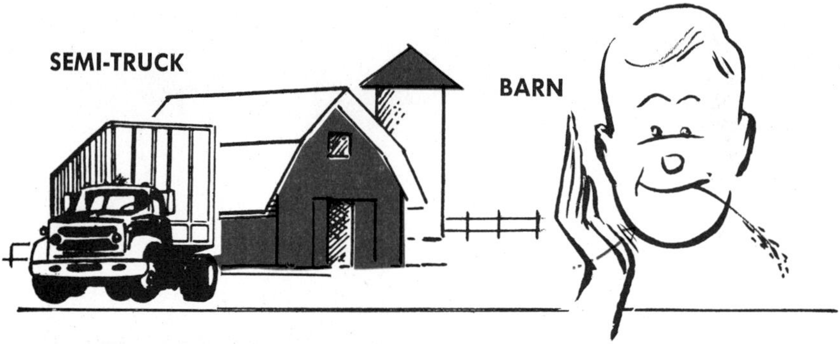

SEMI-TRUCK

BARN

OCCUPATION

The FARMER

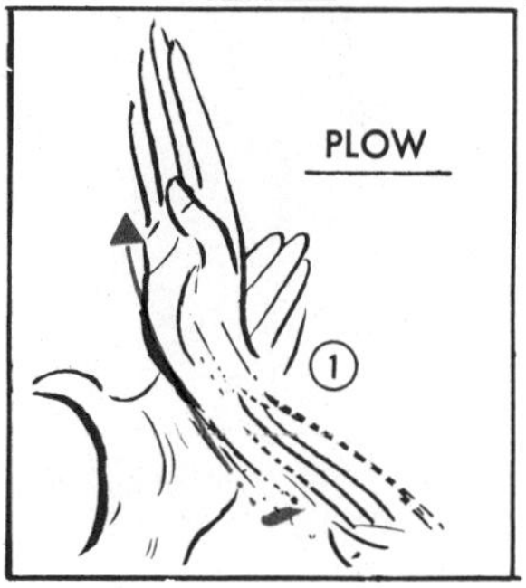

PLOW

A FARMER is a plower.

The TRUCK

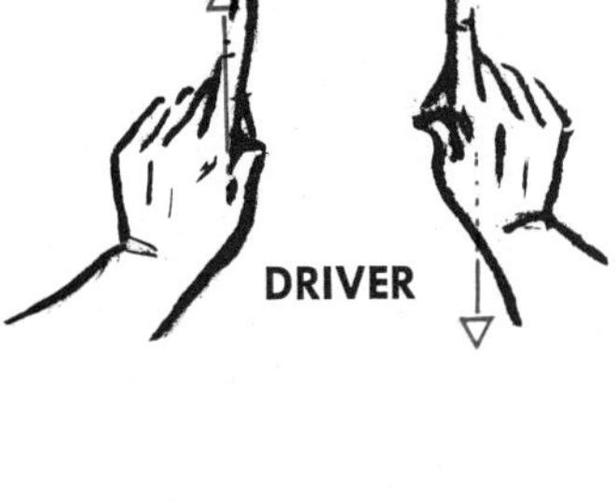

DRIVER

TRACTOR

465

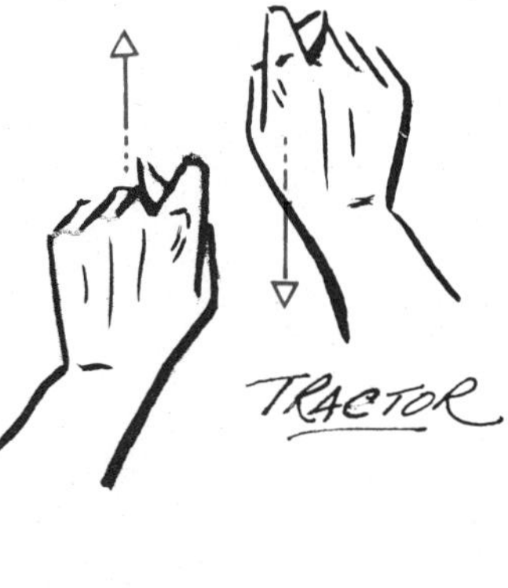

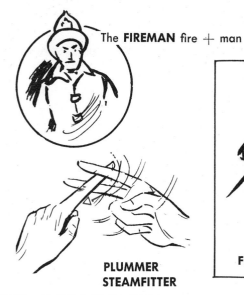

The **FIREMAN** fire + man

FIRE CHIEF

PLUMMER STEAMFITTER

The **PATROLMAN**

**POLICEMAN ("COP")
SHERIFF**
(Officers of the law)

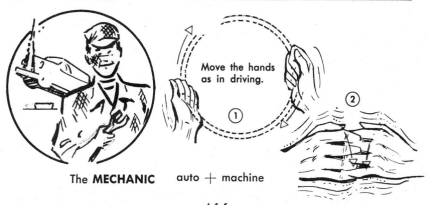

The **MECHANIC** auto + machine

Move the hands as in driving.

① ②

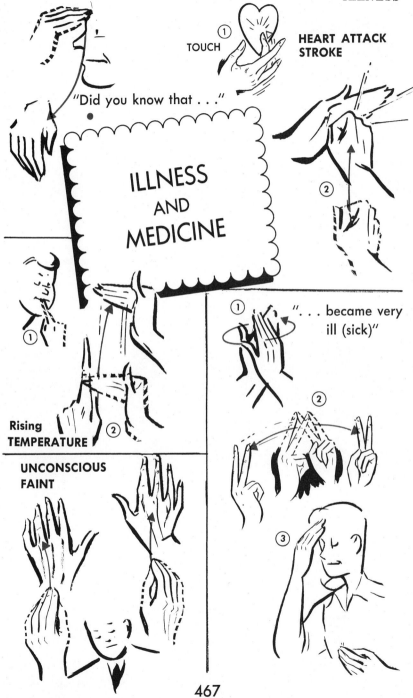

TOUCH ①

HEART ATTACK STROKE

"Did you know that . . ."

ILLNESS
AND
MEDICINE

②

Rising
TEMPERATURE

①
②

① "... became very ill (sick)"

②

③

UNCONSCIOUS FAINT

467

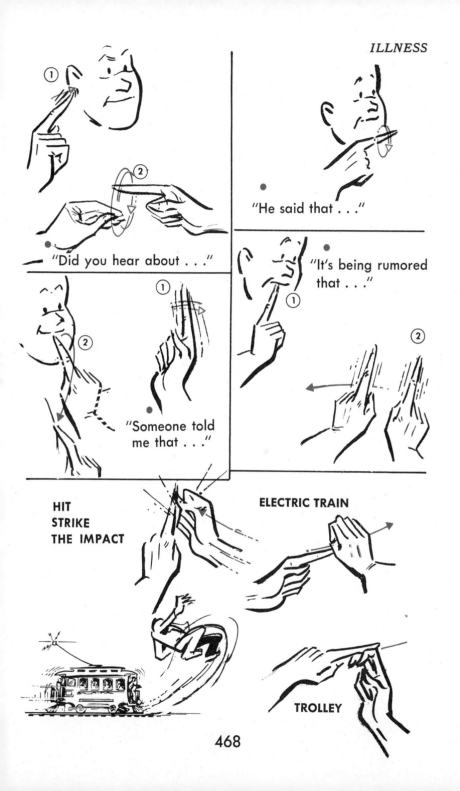

ILLNESS

"He said that . . ."

"Did you hear about . . ."

"It's being rumored that . . ."

"Someone told me that . . ."

HIT
STRIKE
THE IMPACT

ELECTRIC TRAIN

TROLLEY

468

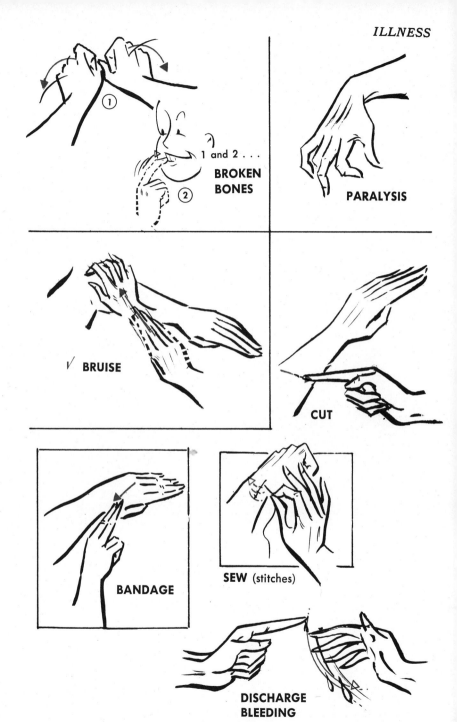

PARALYSIS

1 and 2 . . .
BROKEN BONES

V **BRUISE**

CUT

BANDAGE

SEW (stitches)

DISCHARGE BLEEDING

469

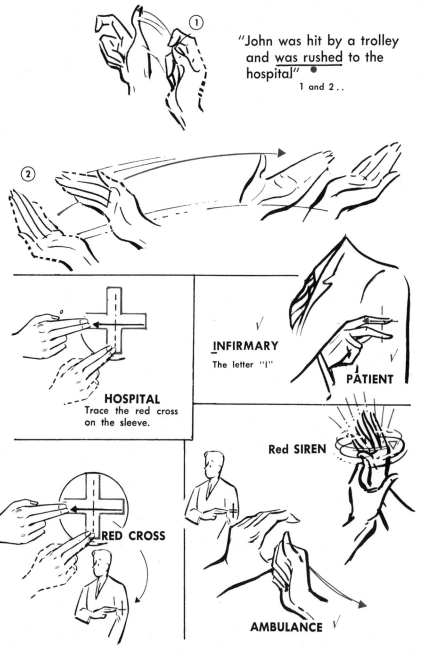

"John was hit by a trolley and <u>was rushed</u> to the hospital"

1 and 2..

HOSPITAL
Trace the red cross on the sleeve.

INFIRMARY
The letter "I"

PATIENT

RED CROSS

Red SIREN

AMBULANCE

470

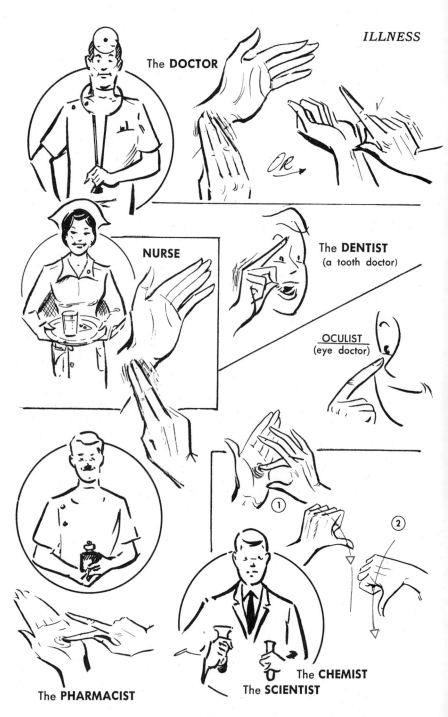

The **DOCTOR**

OR

NURSE

The **DENTIST**
(a tooth doctor)

OCULIST
(eye doctor)

1

2

The **PHARMACIST**

The **CHEMIST**
The **SCIENTIST**

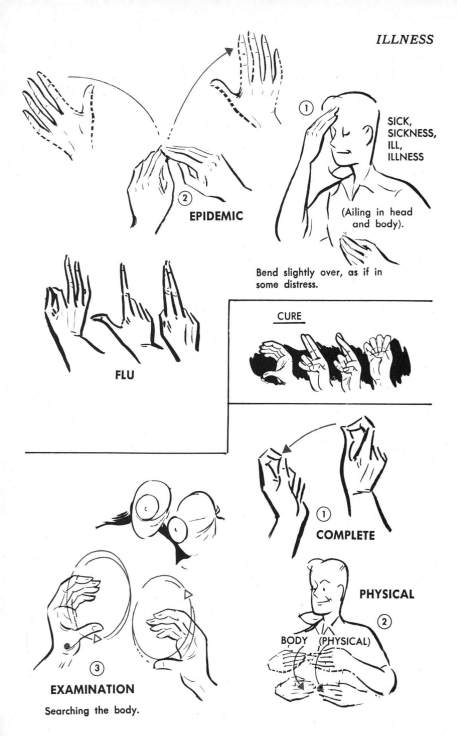

EPIDEMIC

SICK,
SICKNESS,
ILL,
ILLNESS

(Ailing in head
and body).

Bend slightly over, as if in
some distress.

FLU

CURE

COMPLETE

PHYSICAL

BODY (PHYSICAL)

EXAMINATION

Searching the body.

472

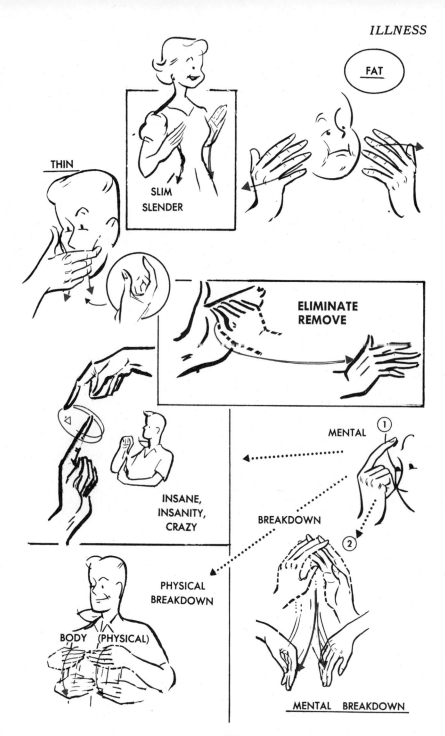

FAT

SLIM
SLENDER

THIN

ELIMINATE
REMOVE

INSANE,
INSANITY,
CRAZY

MENTAL ①

BREAKDOWN ②

PHYSICAL
BREAKDOWN

BODY (PHYSICAL)

MENTAL BREAKDOWN

473

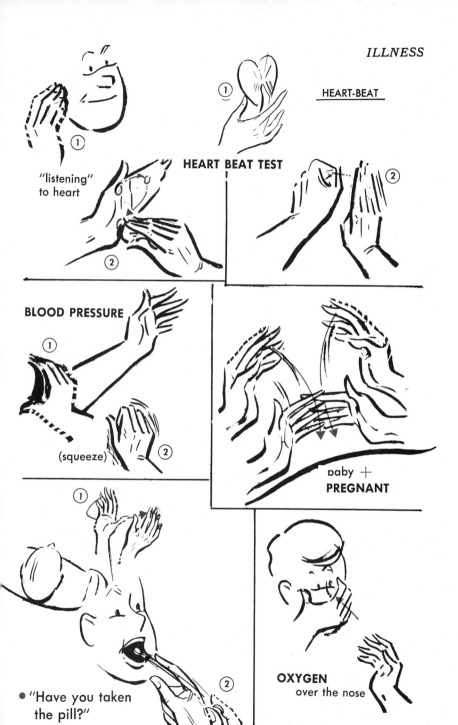

HEART-BEAT

"listening"
to heart

HEART BEAT TEST

BLOOD PRESSURE

(squeeze)

baby +
PREGNANT

• "Have you taken
the pill?"

OXYGEN
over the nose

474

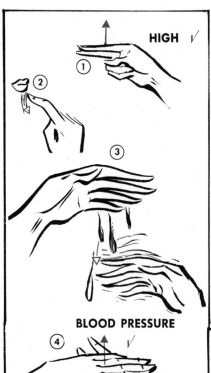

HIGH √

BLOOD PRESSURE

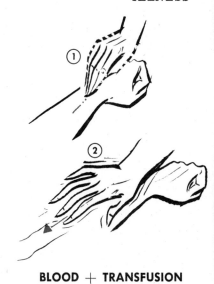

BLOOD + TRANSFUSION

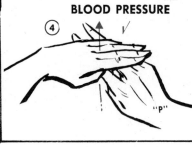

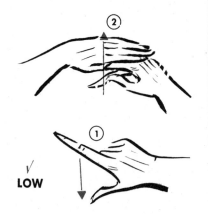

LOW √

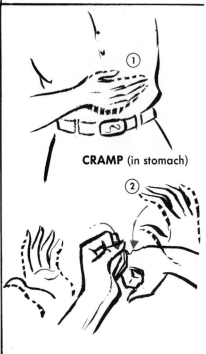

CRAMP (in stomach)

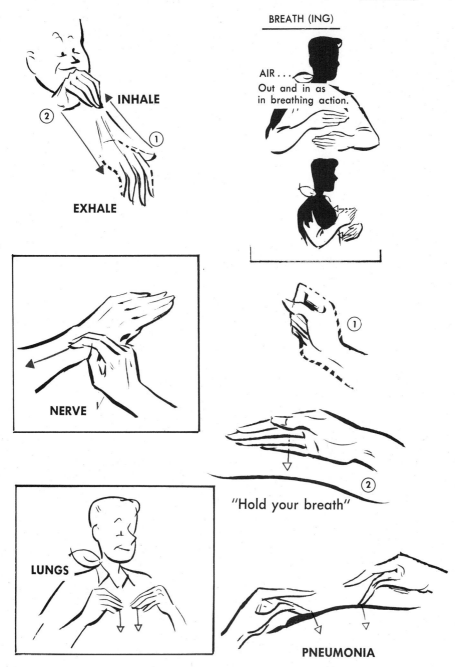

INHALE

② ①

EXHALE

BREATH (ING)

AIR . . .
Out and in as
in breathing action.

NERVE

① ②

"Hold your breath"

LUNGS

PNEUMONIA

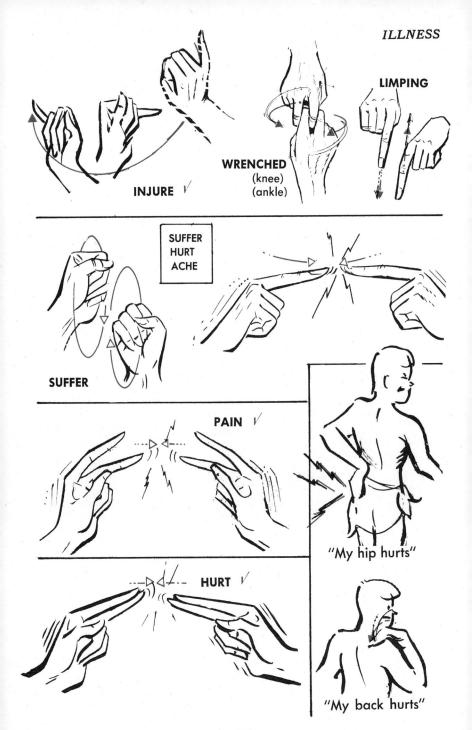

LIMPING

INJURE

WRENCHED
(knee)
(ankle)

SUFFER
HURT
ACHE

SUFFER

PAIN

"My hip hurts"

HURT

"My back hurts"

477

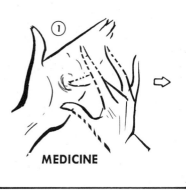

① **MEDICINE**

MEDICAL SCIENCE

② move hands alternately

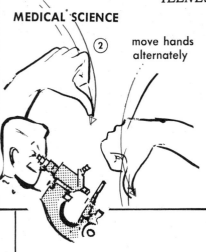

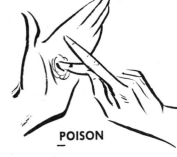

POISON

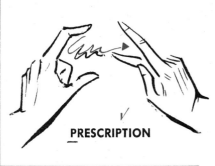

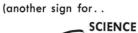

PRESCRIPTION

alternate movements

LAB (spell)

(another sign for. .

SCIENCE

"C"
CHEMISTRY

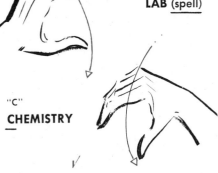

EXPERIMENT
The letter "E"

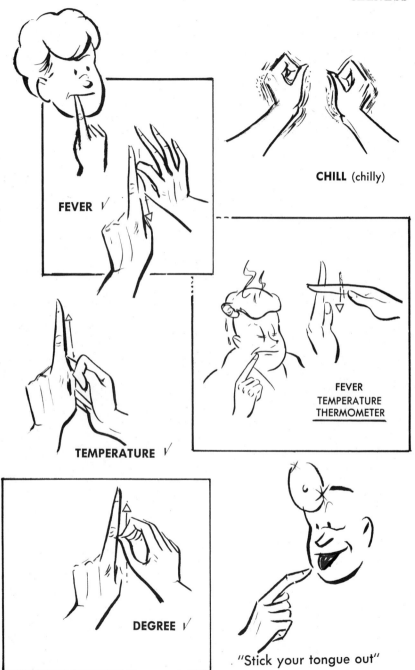

FEVER √

CHILL (chilly)

TEMPERATURE √

FEVER
TEMPERATURE
THERMOMETER

DEGREE √

"Stick your tongue out"

479

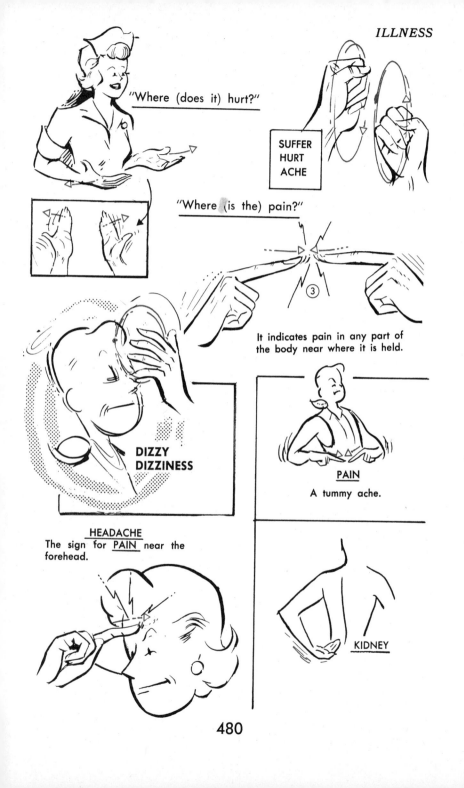

"Where (does it) hurt?"

SUFFER
HURT
ACHE

"Where (is the) pain?"

③

It indicates pain in any part of the body near where it is held.

**DIZZY
DIZZINESS**

<u>PAIN</u>
A tummy ache.

<u>HEADACHE</u>
The sign for <u>PAIN</u> near the forehead.

<u>KIDNEY</u>

480

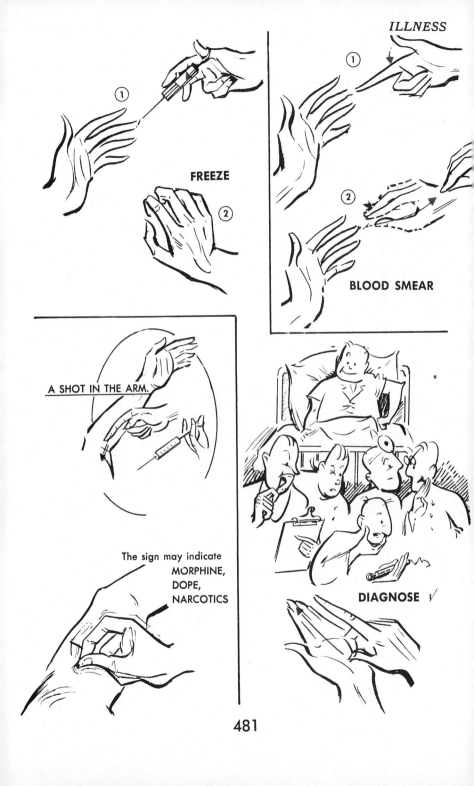

ILLNESS

FREEZE

BLOOD SMEAR

A SHOT IN THE ARM.

The sign may indicate
MORPHINE,
DOPE,
NARCOTICS

DIAGNOSE √

481

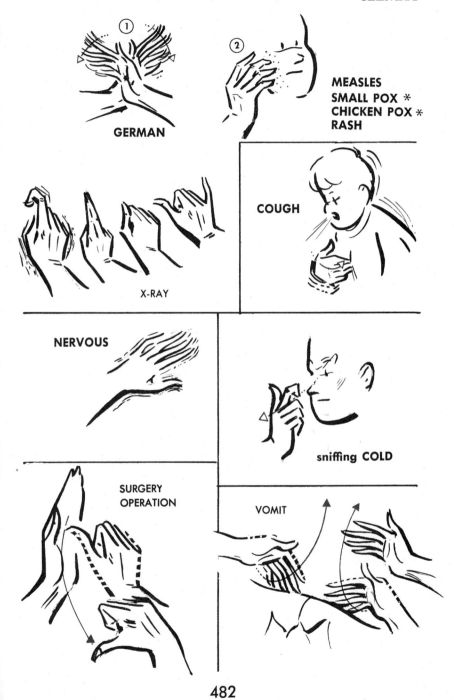

GERMAN

**MEASLES
SMALL POX** ✳
CHICKEN POX ✳
RASH

X-RAY

COUGH

NERVOUS

sniffing **COLD**

**SURGERY
OPERATION**

VOMIT

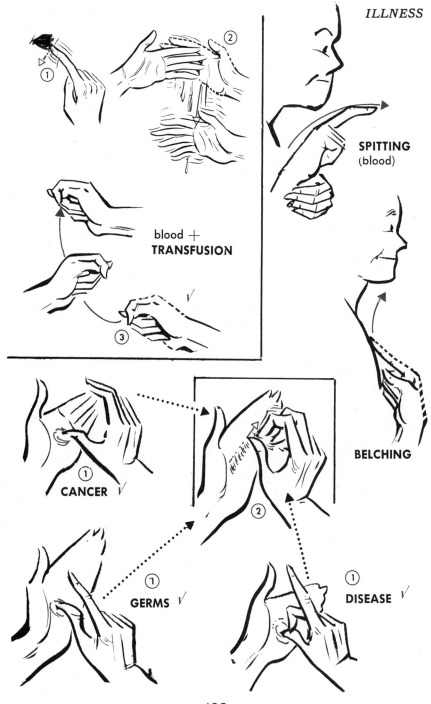

SPITTING
(blood)

blood +
TRANSFUSION

BELCHING

CANCER

GERMS

DISEASE

483

CHURCH
CHAPEL

RELIGION

CHURCH

TEMPLE
The letter "T"

Religion

GOD

WORSHIP

GOD'S

WORD

SAVIOR

484

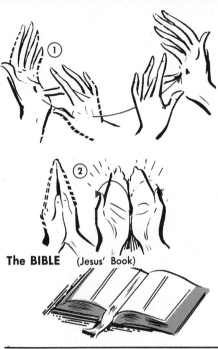

The BIBLE (Jesus' Book)

BIBLE . . . as if received from God

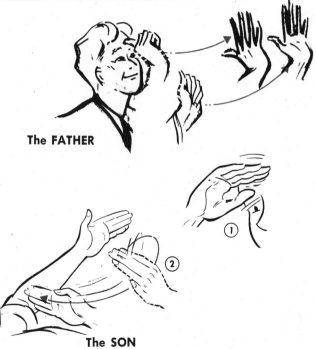

The FATHER

The SON

485

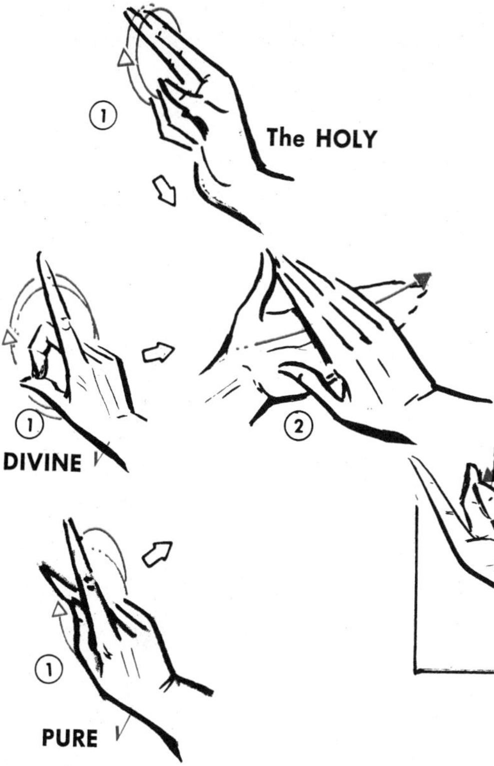

The HOLY

①

②

DIVINE

①
①

PURE

①

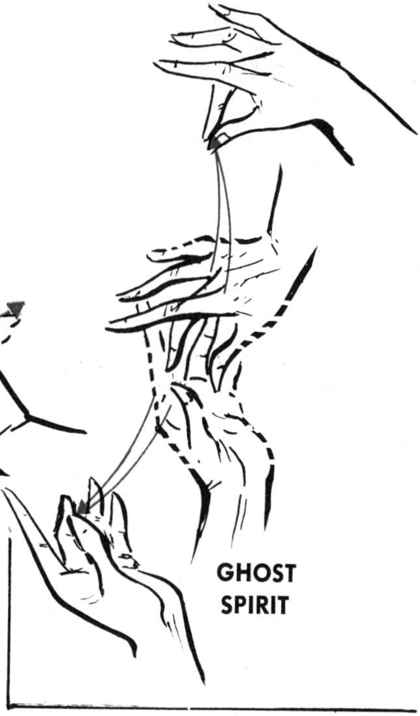

GHOST
SPIRIT

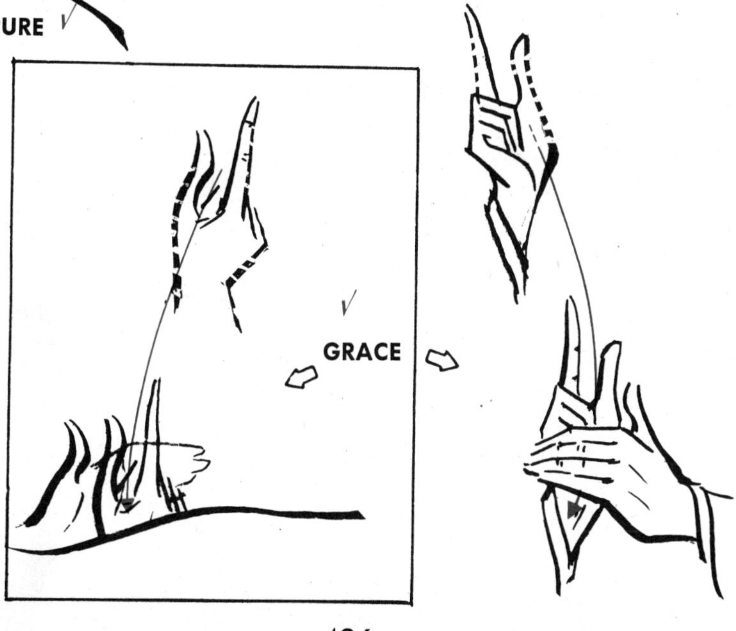

GRACE

486

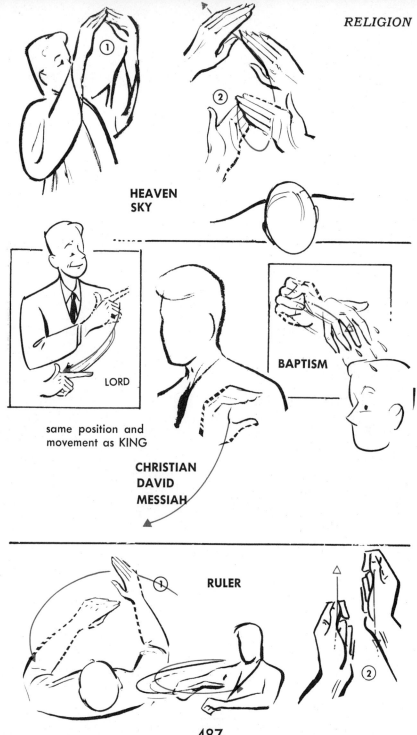

HEAVEN
SKY

LORD

same position and
movement as KING

BAPTISM

CHRISTIAN
DAVID
MESSIAH

RULER

487

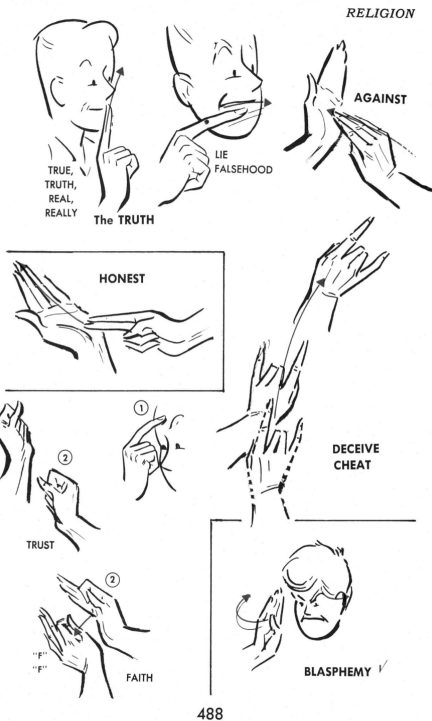

AGAINST

TRUE,
TRUTH,
REAL,
REALLY

The **TRUTH**

LIE
FALSEHOOD

HONEST

**DECEIVE
CHEAT**

① ②

TRUST

② "F" "F" **FAITH**

BLASPHEMY ✓

488

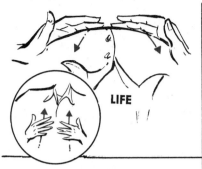

LIFE

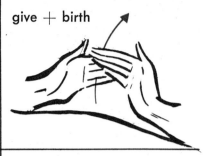

give + birth

LIVE

ENGAGEMENT

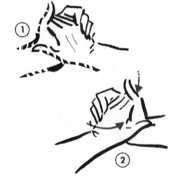

① ②

PEACE

MARRIAGE

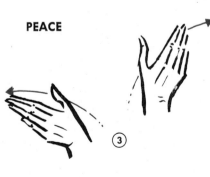

③

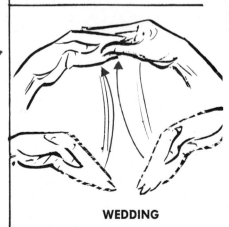

WEDDING

489

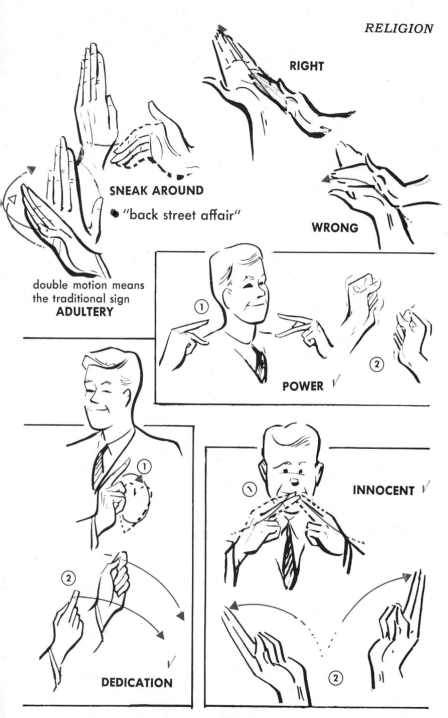

RIGHT

SNEAK AROUND

● "back street affair"

WRONG

double motion means
the traditional sign
ADULTERY

① ② **POWER** ✓

INNOCENT ✓

① ②

① ② **DEDICATION** ✓

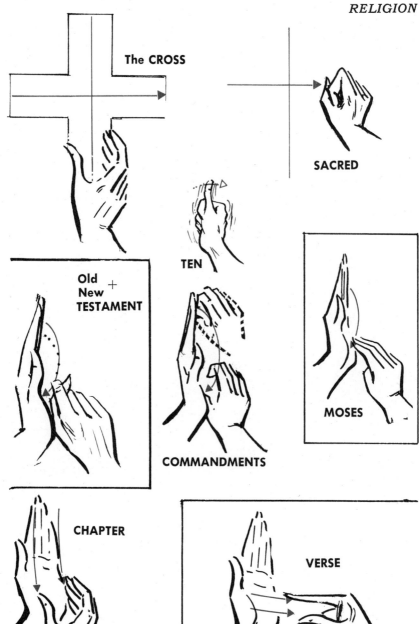

The CROSS

SACRED

TEN

Old
New + TESTAMENT

COMMANDMENTS

MOSES

CHAPTER

VERSE

491

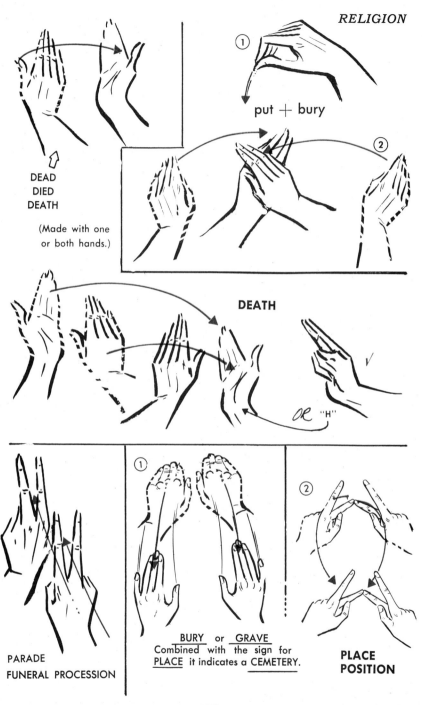

RELIGION

① put + bury

②

DEAD
DIED
DEATH

(Made with one
or both hands.)

DEATH

or "H"

PARADE
FUNERAL PROCESSION

① BURY or GRAVE
Combined with the sign for
PLACE it indicates a CEMETERY.

② PLACE
POSITION

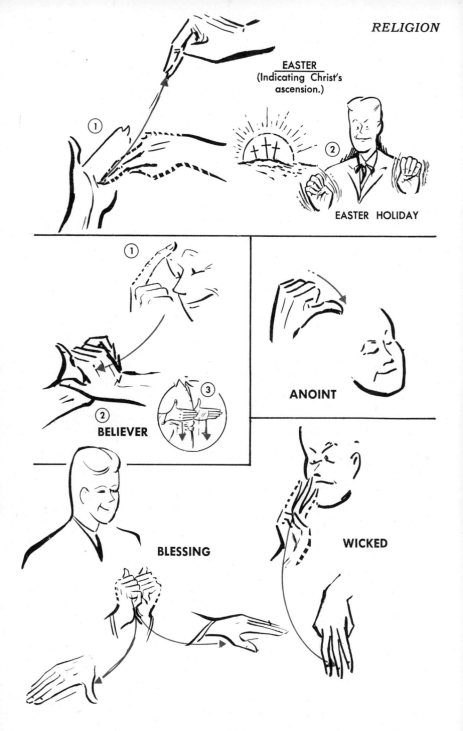

EASTER
(Indicating Christ's ascension.)

EASTER HOLIDAY

BELIEVER

ANOINT

BLESSING

WICKED

"What

Church (religion)

do you
*

"What Church (religion)
do you  belong?"

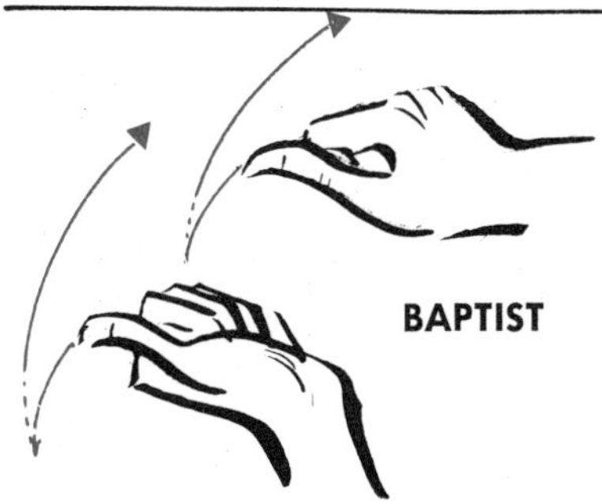

belong?"

BAPTIST

CATHOLIC

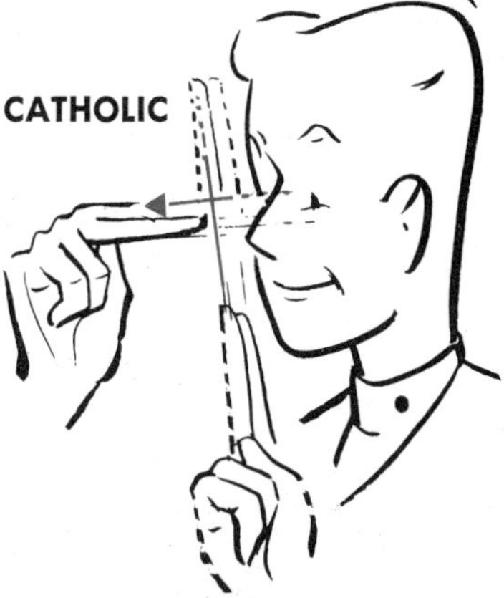

LUTHERAN (Synod)

JEHOVAH WITNESS

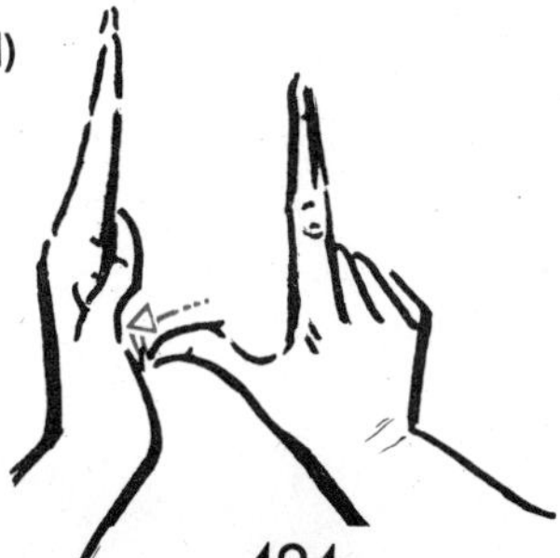

LUTHERAN

494

ASSEMBLY of GOD

EPISCOPALIAN

PASSOVER

SEVENTH DAY ADVENT spell: **SDA**
UNITED BRETHREN **UB**
CHURCH of GOD

PRESBYTERIAN

MORMON

METHODIST

KNEEL

METHODIST

495

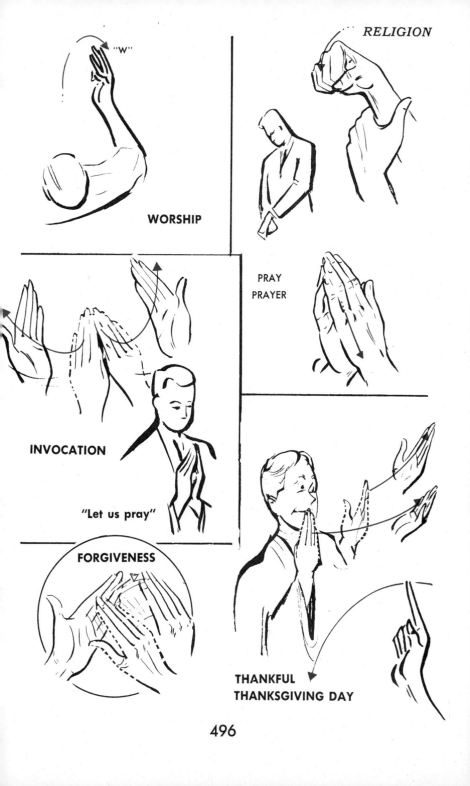

"W"

WORSHIP

RELIGION

PRAY
PRAYER

INVOCATION

"Let us pray"

FORGIVENESS

THANKFUL
THANKSGIVING DAY

ANGEL

**PROPHET
FORECAST**

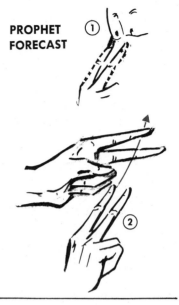

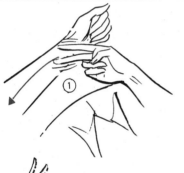

DESTRUCTION

SHEPHERD

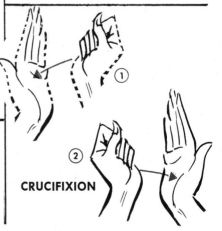

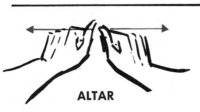

ALTAR

CRUCIFIXION

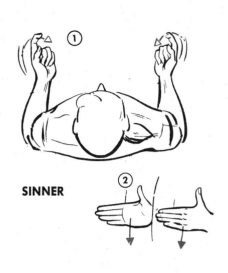

CHRISTMAS

Literally, Jesus' birthday. This is the correct formal sign for CHRISTMAS. However, in common usage we use the sign above, indicating SANTA CLAUS.

SINNER

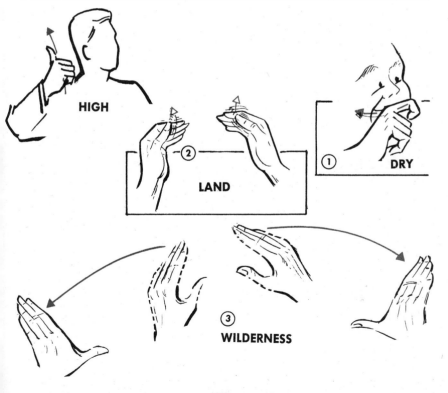

HIGH

LAND

DRY

WILDERNESS

498

ISRAEL

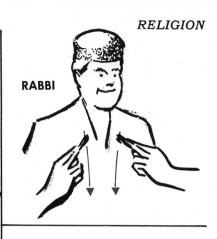

RABBI

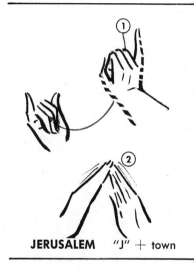

JERUSALEM "J" + town

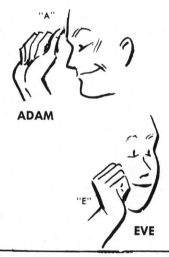

ADAM

EVE

MIRACLE

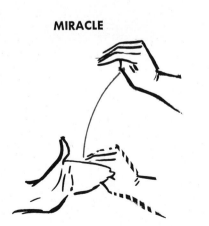

JEWISH HEBREW

YAHWEH (Jewish Holiday)

499

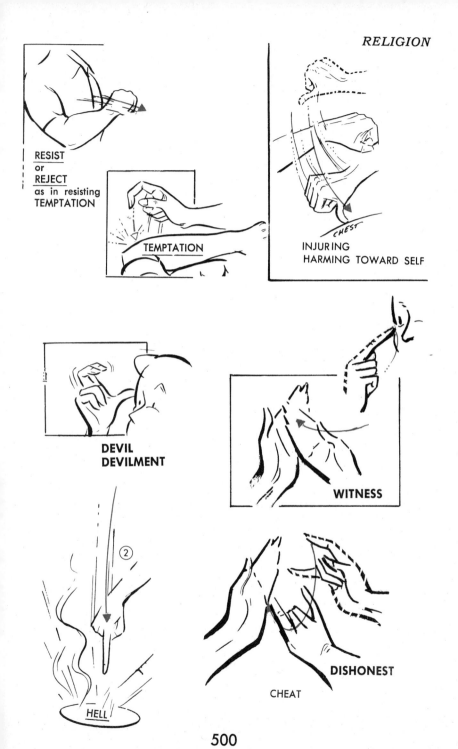

RESIST
or
REJECT
as in resisting
TEMPTATION

TEMPTATION

CHEST

INJURING
HARMING TOWARD SELF

DEVIL
DEVILMENT

WITNESS

②

HELL

DISHONEST

CHEAT

500

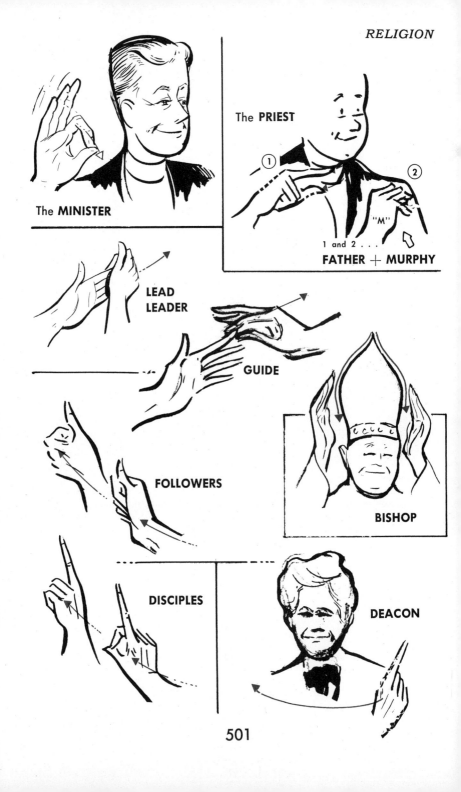

The **MINISTER**

The **PRIEST**

①

②

"M"

1 and 2 . . .
FATHER + MURPHY

**LEAD
LEADER**

GUIDE

FOLLOWERS

BISHOP

DISCIPLES

DEACON

501

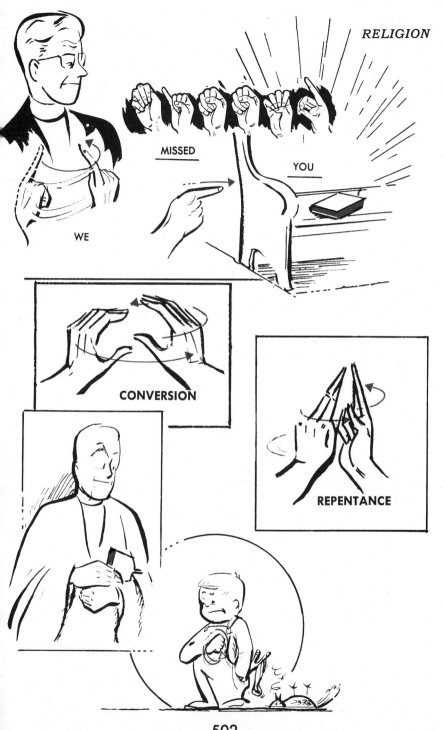

WE

MISSED

YOU

CONVERSION

REPENTANCE

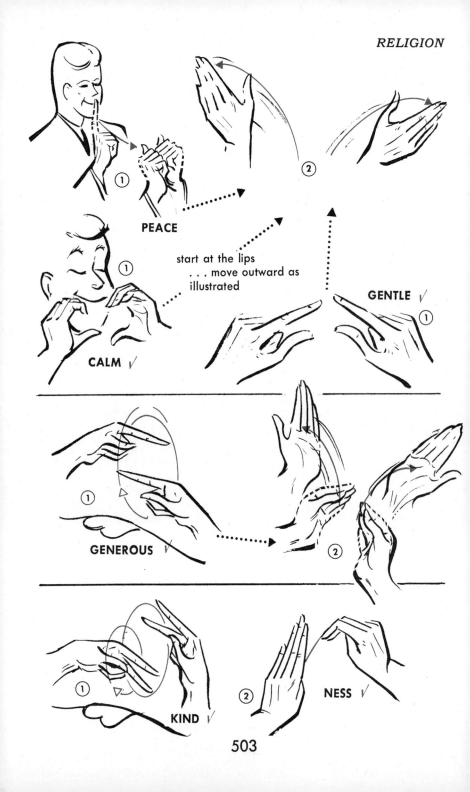

PEACE

start at the lips
. . . move outward as
illustrated

GENTLE √

CALM √

GENEROUS √

KIND √

NESS √

503

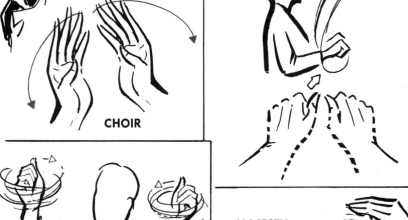

CHOIR

SACRIFICE

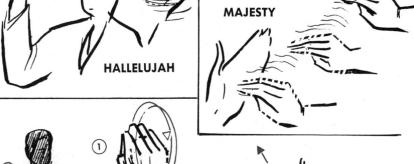

HALLELUJAH

MAJESTY

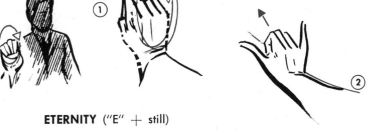

ETERNITY ("E" + still)

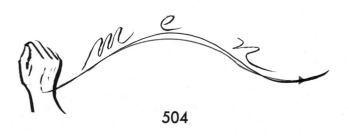

SOUL

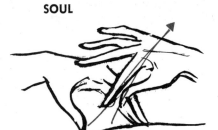

TABERNACLE √

DOCTRINE like "teacher"

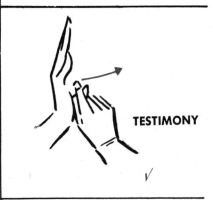

TESTIMONY

√

GOSPEL √

SAINT √

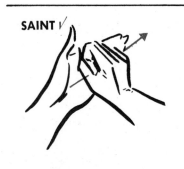

SEMINARY

"Our Father"

Our Father who art in heaven,
  hallowed be thy name.
Thy kingdom come, thy will be done
  on earth, as it is in heaven.
Give us this day our daily bread.
And forgive us our debts, as we also
  forgive our debtors.
And lead us not into temptation, but
  deliver us from evil.
For thine is the kingdom, and the
  power, and the glory, forever.
Amen.

Our

Father   who   art

in   heaven,

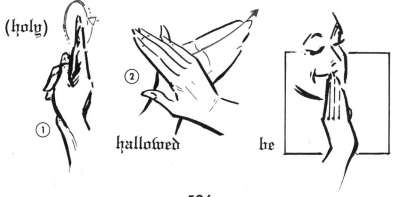

(holy)

hallowed   be

506

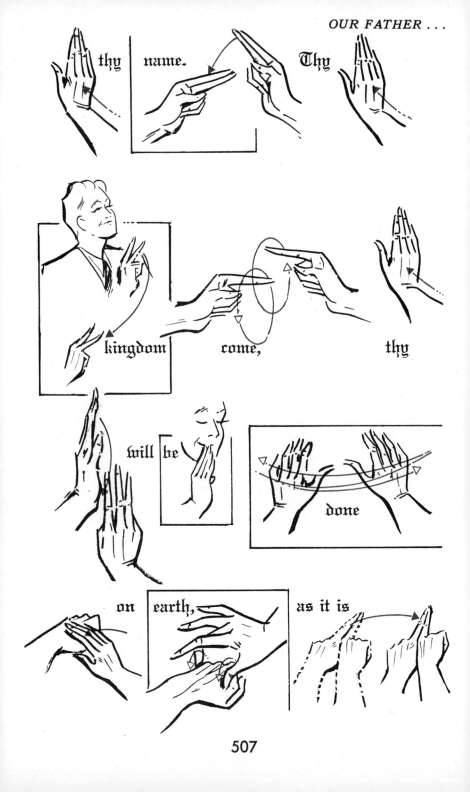

thy | name. | Thy

kingdom | come, | thy

will be | done

on | earth, | as it is

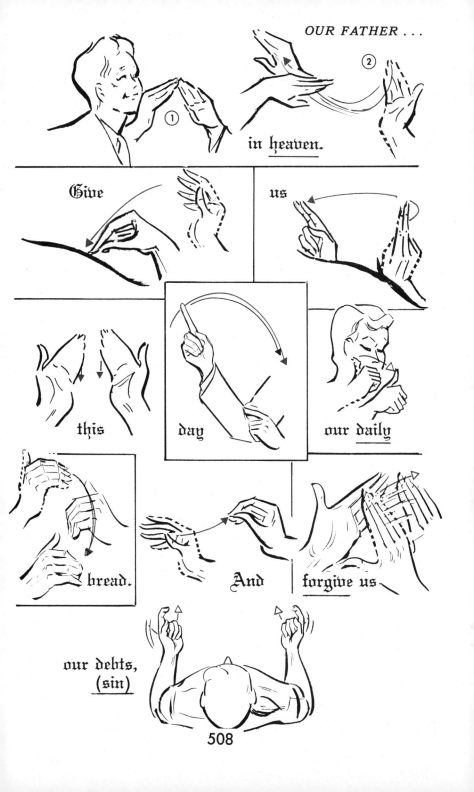

OUR FATHER . . .

in heaven.

Give us

this day our daily

bread. And forgive us

our debts, (sin)

508

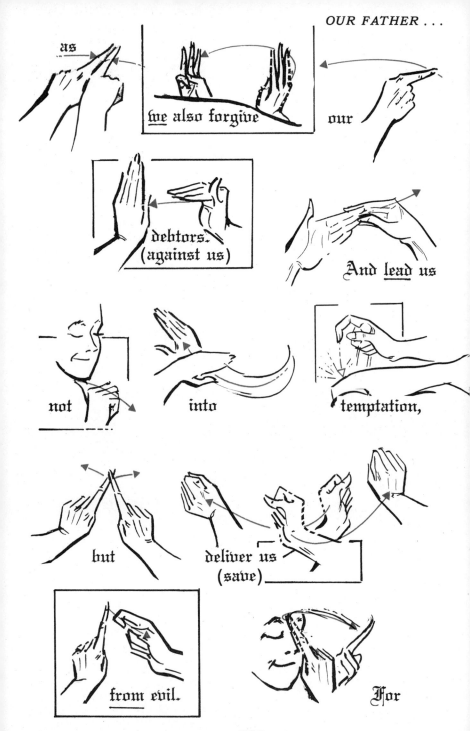

as

we also forgive

our

debtors.
(against us)

And lead us

not

into

temptation,

but

deliver us
(save)

from evil.

For

509

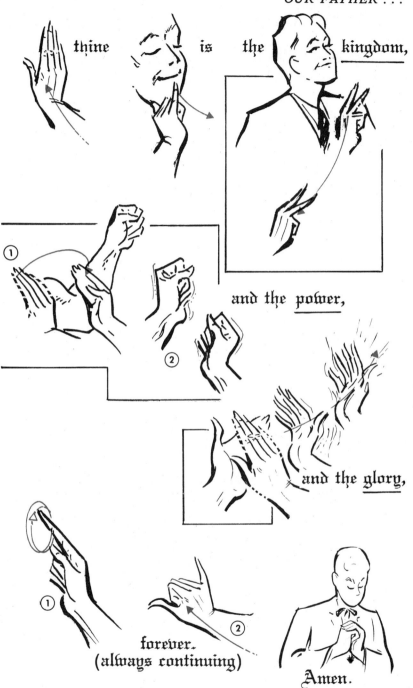

thine is the kingdom,

and the power,

and the glory,

forever.
(always continuing)

Amen.

"JESUS LOVES ME"

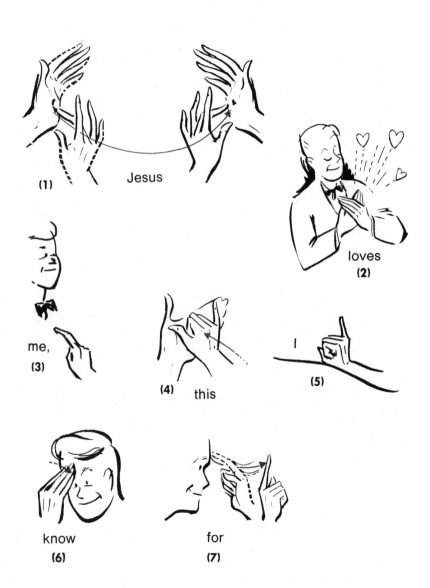

(1) Jesus

loves
(2)

me,
(3)

(4)   this

(5)

know
(6)

for
(7)

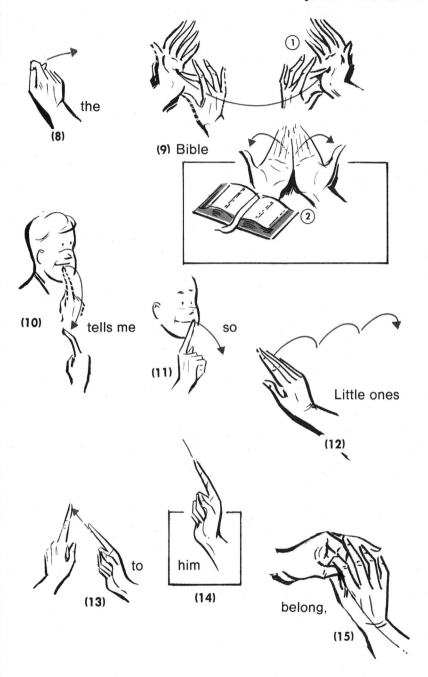

the (8)

(9) Bible

tells me (10)

so (11)

Little ones (12)

to (13)

him (14)

belong, (15)

512

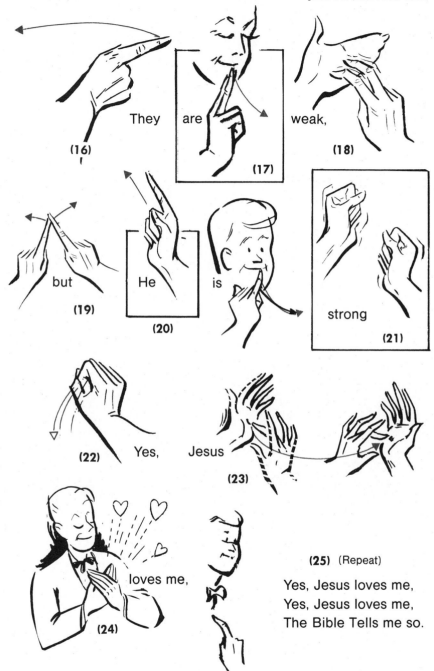

They (16)

are (17)

weak, (18)

but (19)

He (20)

is

strong (21)

Yes, (22)

Jesus (23)

loves me, (24)

(25) (Repeat)

Yes, Jesus loves me,
Yes, Jesus loves me,
The Bible Tells me so.

513

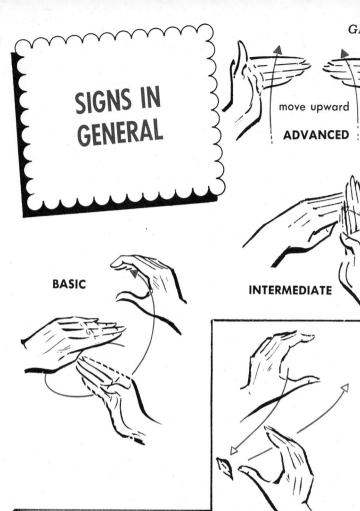

SIGNS IN GENERAL

GENERAL

move upward

ADVANCED

INTERMEDIATE

BASIC

COMMUNICATION

INTERVIEW

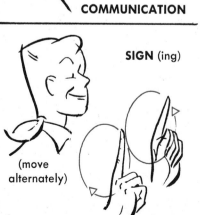

SIGN (ing)

(move alternately)

514

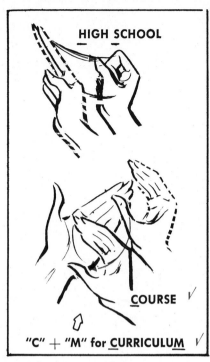

HIGH SCHOOL

COURSE √

"C" + "M" for CURRICULUM √

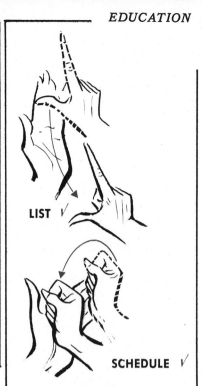

LIST √

SCHEDULE √

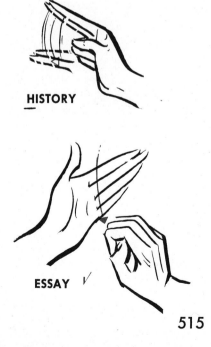

HISTORY

PUPIL

ESSAY √

PAGE √

515

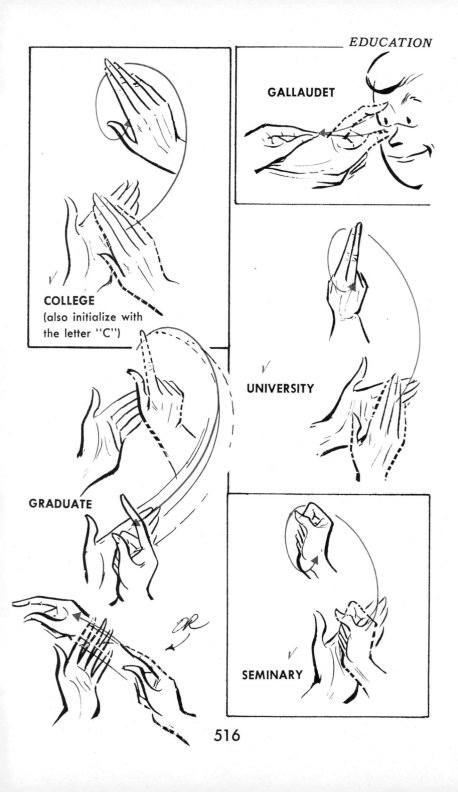

EDUCATION

GALLAUDET

COLLEGE
(also initialize with
the letter "C")

UNIVERSITY

GRADUATE

OR

SEMINARY

516

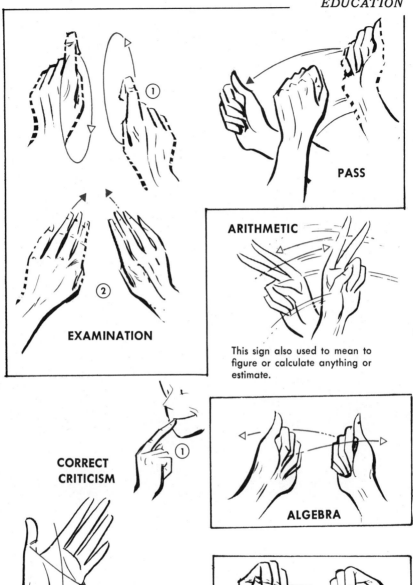

PASS

EXAMINATION

ARITHMETIC

This sign also used to mean to figure or calculate anything or estimate.

CORRECT CRITICISM

ALGEBRA

MATHEMATICS

517

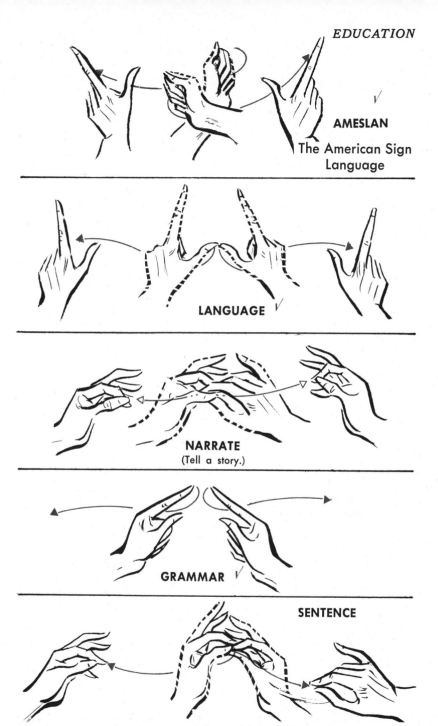

AMESLAN

The American Sign Language

LANGUAGE

NARRATE

(Tell a story.)

GRAMMAR

SENTENCE

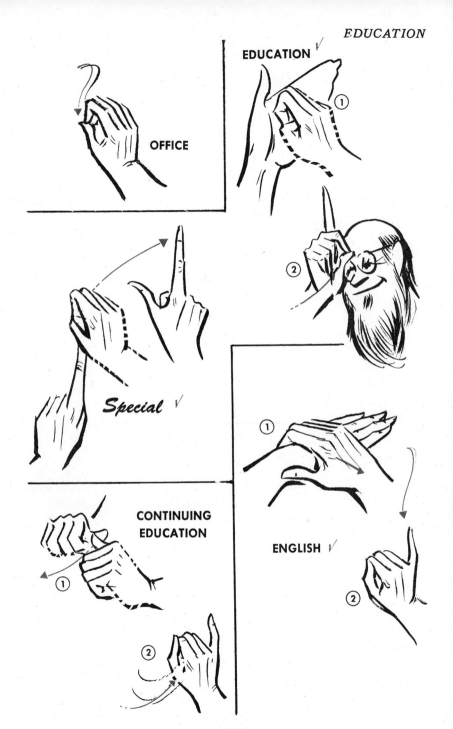

OFFICE

EDUCATION

Special

CONTINUING
EDUCATION

ENGLISH

519

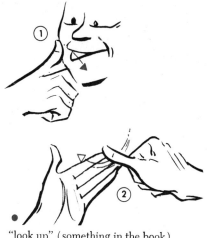

① ②

"look up" (something in the book)
pantomime: thumbing through the pages

LITERATURE √

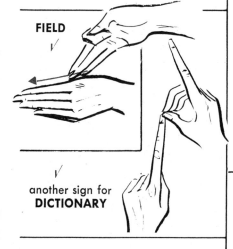

FIELD √

another sign for
DICTIONARY √

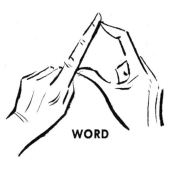

WORD

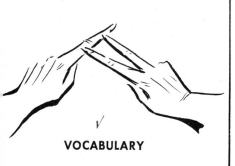

VOCABULARY √

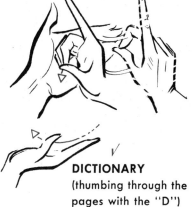

DICTIONARY √
(thumbing through the
pages with the "D")

520

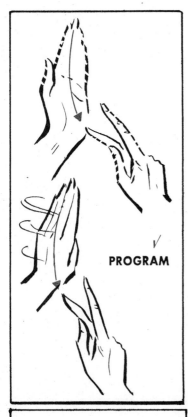

PROGRAM

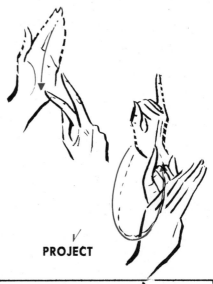

PROJECT

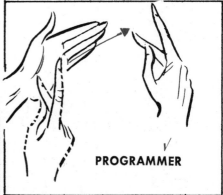

PROGRAMMER

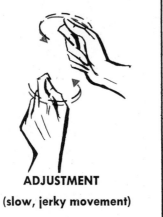

ADJUSTMENT

(slow, jerky movement)

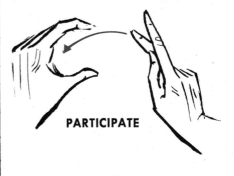

PARTICIPATE

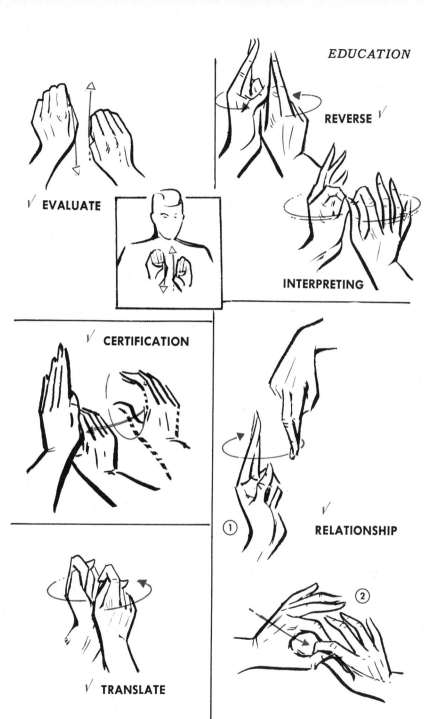

EDUCATION

REVERSE √

√ EVALUATE

INTERPRETING

√ CERTIFICATION

①

√ RELATIONSHIP

②

√ TRANSLATE

522

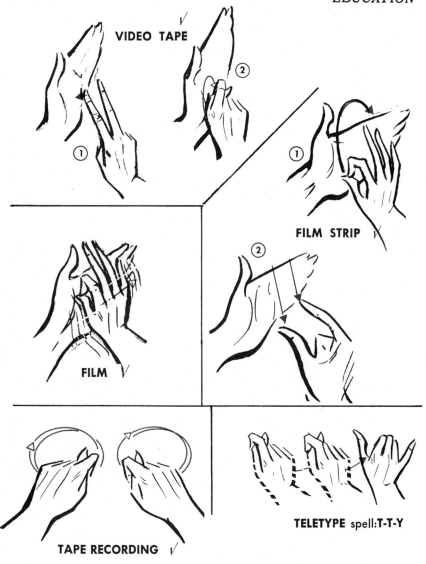

VIDEO TAPE

FILM STRIP

FILM

TAPE RECORDING

TELETYPE spell:**T-T-Y**

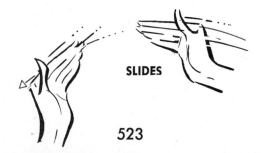

SLIDES

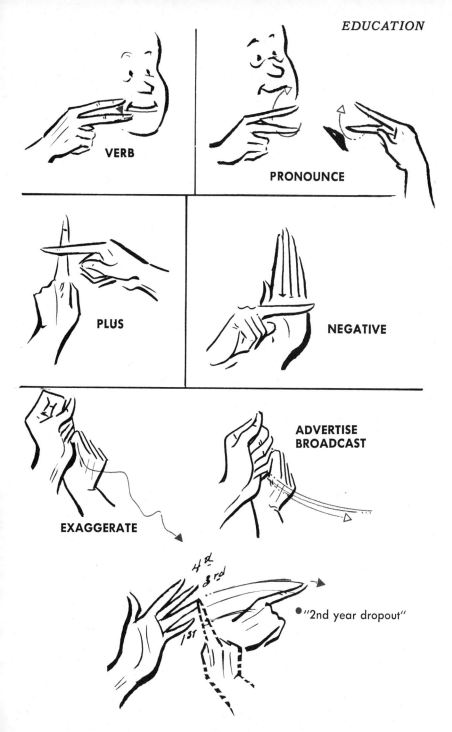

VERB

PRONOUNCE

PLUS

NEGATIVE

ADVERTISE
BROADCAST

EXAGGERATE

•"2nd year dropout"

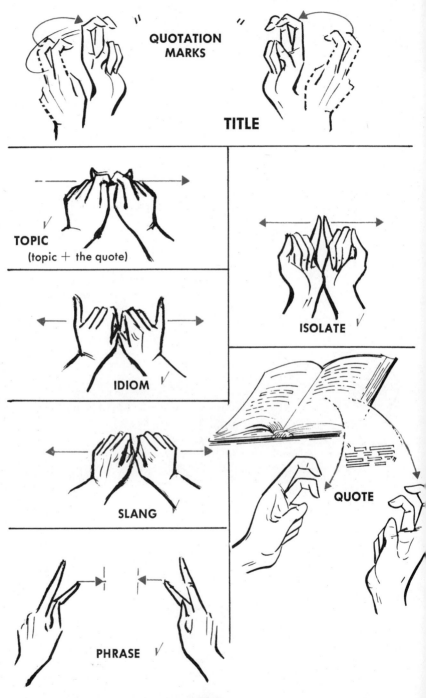

QUOTATION MARKS

TITLE

TOPIC
(topic + the quote)

ISOLATE

IDIOM

SLANG

QUOTE

PHRASE

525

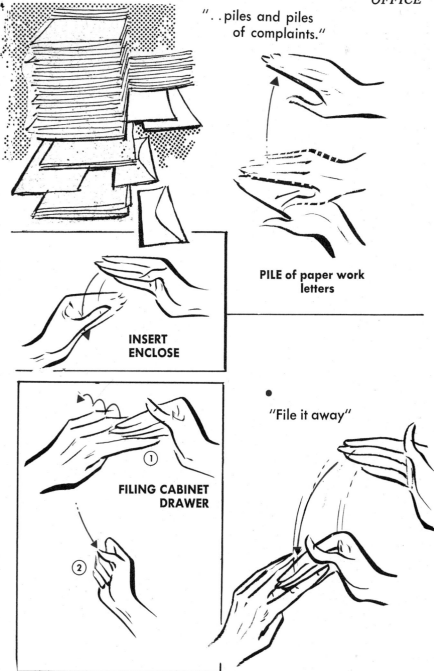

". . piles and piles of complaints."

PILE of paper work letters

INSERT ENCLOSE

FILING CABINET DRAWER

① ②

"File it away"

526

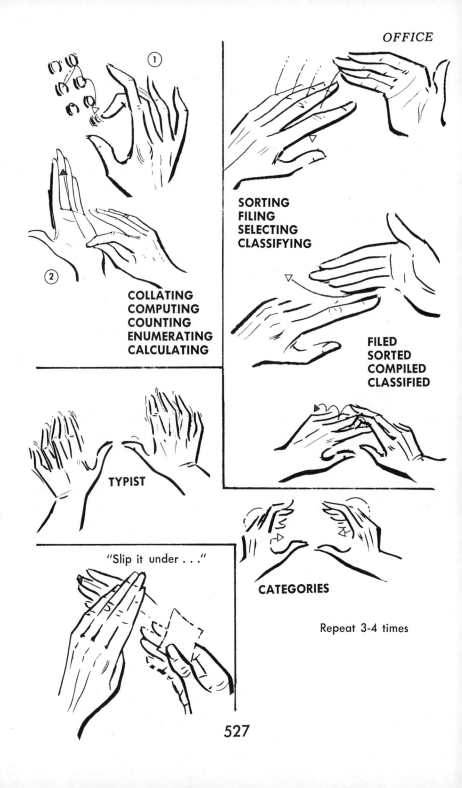

① ②

SORTING
FILING
SELECTING
CLASSIFYING

COLLATING
COMPUTING
COUNTING
ENUMERATING
CALCULATING

FILED
SORTED
COMPILED
CLASSIFIED

TYPIST

CATEGORIES

"Slip it under . . ."

Repeat 3-4 times

527

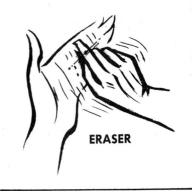

ERASER

PAPER + CLIP

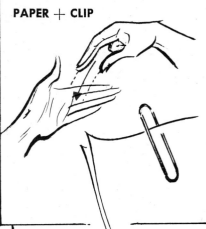

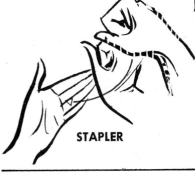

STAPLER

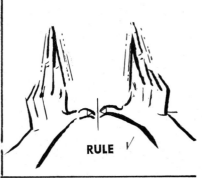

RULE

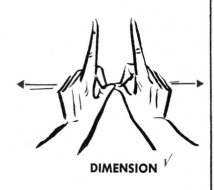

DIMENSION

MAGNIFYING GLASS

528

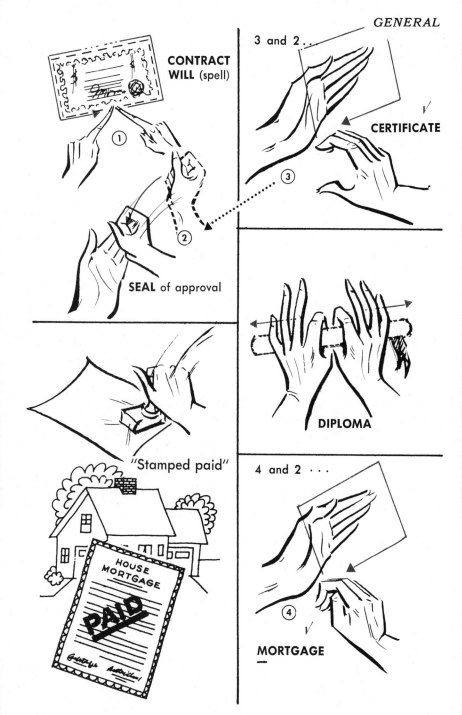

CONTRACT
WILL (spell)

① ②

SEAL of approval

GENERAL

3 and 2 . .

CERTIFICATE

③

DIPLOMA

"Stamped paid"

HOUSE
MORTGAGE

PAID

4 and 2 · · ·

④

MORTGAGE
—

529

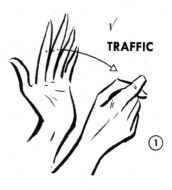

TRAFFIC

①

VIOLATION

②

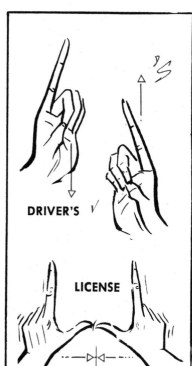

DRIVER'S

LICENSE

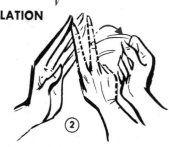

OPERATE
OPERATOR

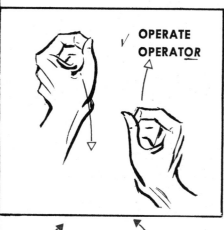

move forward then
backward (slowly)

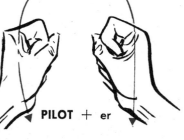

PILOT + er

530

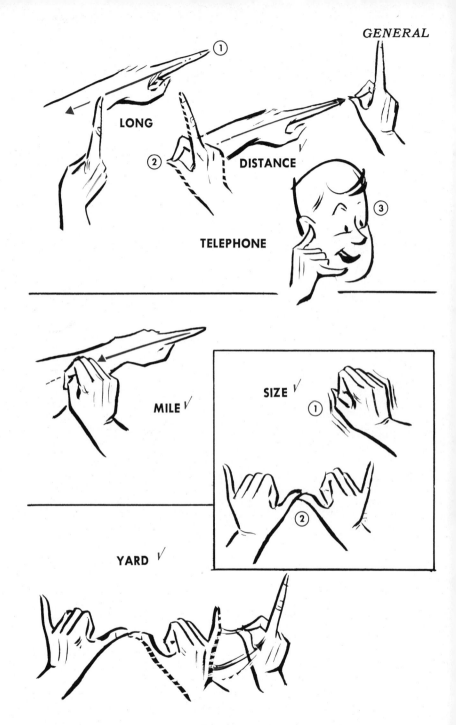

GENERAL

LONG

DISTANCE

TELEPHONE

MILE ✓

SIZE ✓

YARD ✓

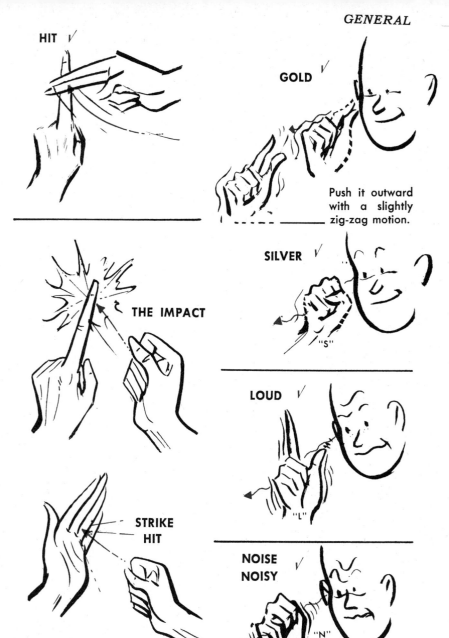

HIT

GOLD

Push it outward with a slightly zig-zag motion.

THE IMPACT

SILVER

"S"

LOUD

"L"

STRIKE
HIT

NOISE
NOISY

"N"

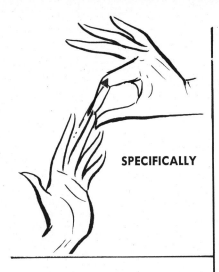

SPECIFICALLY

PROFESSIONAL

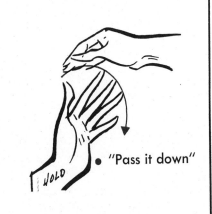

● "Pass it down"

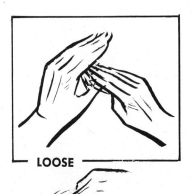

LOOSE

See page 549

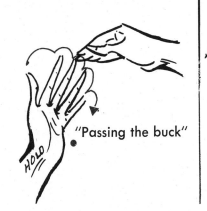

● "Passing the buck"

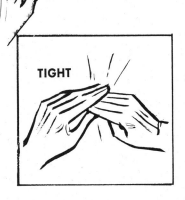

TIGHT

533

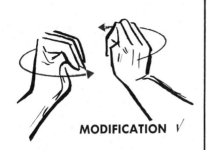

MODIFICATION √

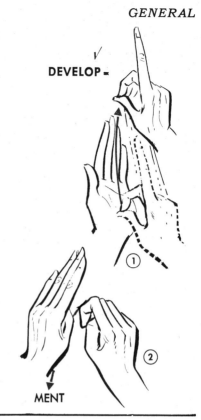

GENERAL

DEVELOP- √

① ②

MENT

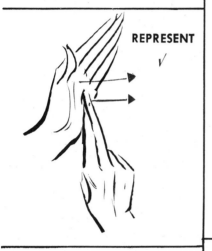

REPRESENT
√

DATA √

INDIVIDUAL √

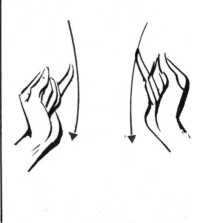

534

CHARACTER

The letter "A"

ATTITUDE

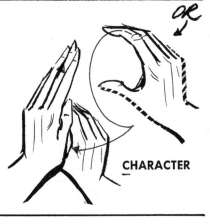

CHARACTER

The letter "B"

"B"

BOSS

FOREMAN

"F"

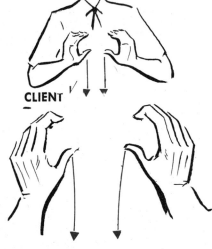

CLIENT

PRACTICE √

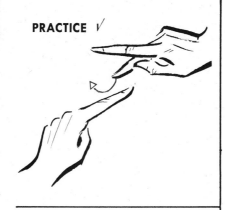

√

PENSION (+ER) ①

(combining with
sign #2 below)

WAGE √

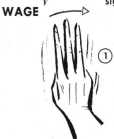

①

TRAINEE (+er) √

INCOME √

①

REHEARSAL √

EARNER

②

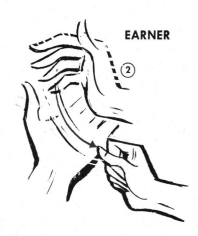

DAY OFF

".. off for the day"

VACATION √

the letter "R" √
for **RETIRE** (ment)

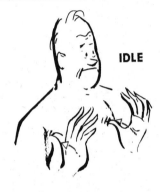

IDLE

REST
RELAX

● "take it easy"

INVOLVE √

AUTHORITY √

537

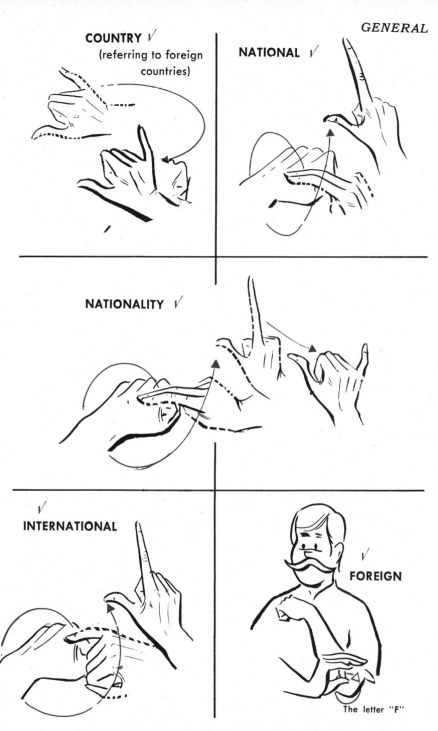

COUNTRY √
(referring to foreign
countries)

GENERAL

NATIONAL √

NATIONALITY √

INTERNATIONAL √

FOREIGN √

The letter "F"

538

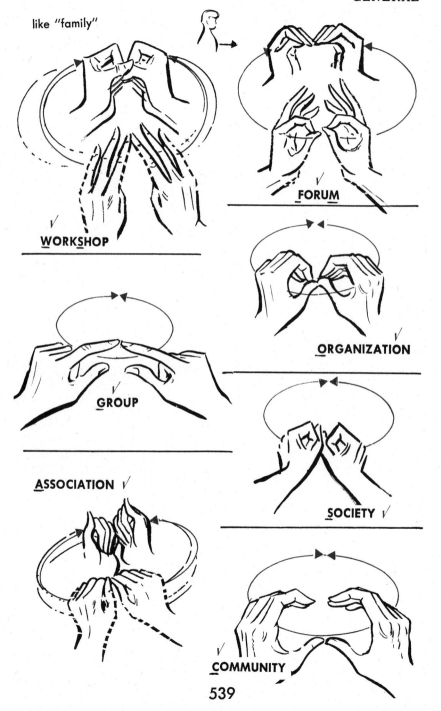

like "family"

WORKSHOP

FORUM

GROUP

ORGANIZATION

ASSOCIATION √

SOCIETY √

COMMUNITY

539

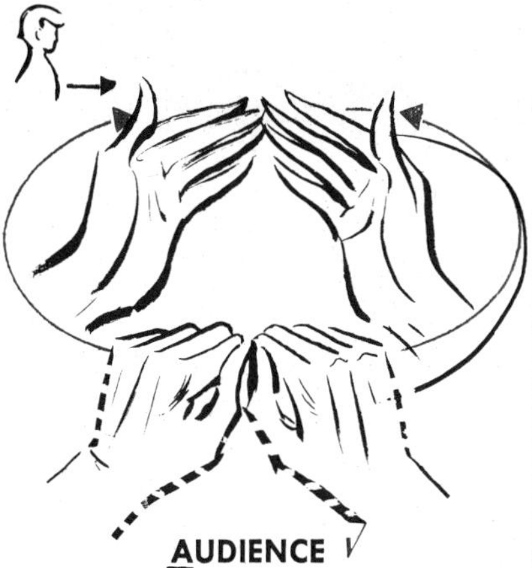

AUDIENCE

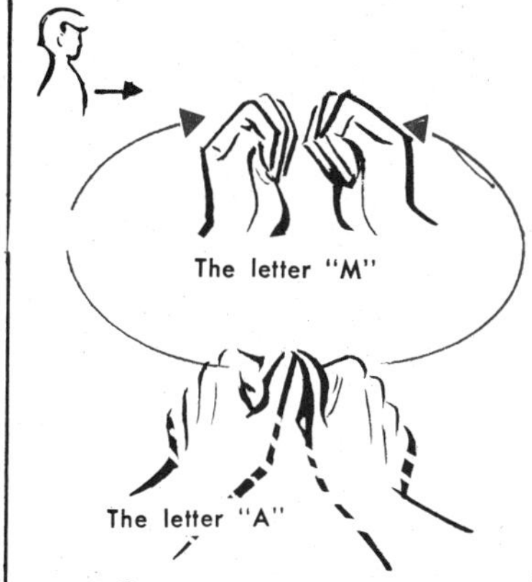

The letter "M"

The letter "A"

AUDITORIUM

OR

Tap on back of hand twice

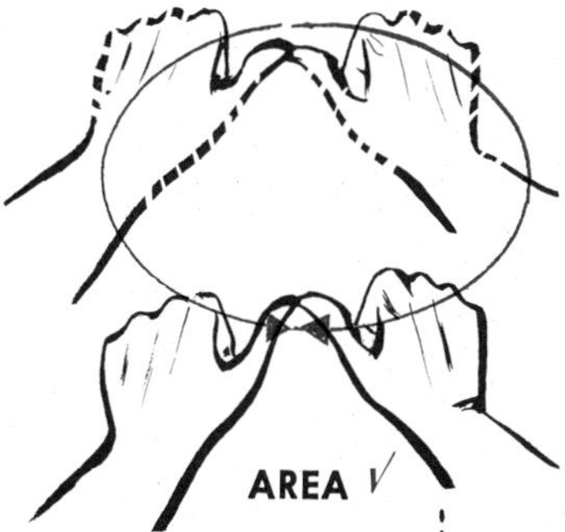

AREA

direction of movement.

SITUATION

CIRCUMSTANCES

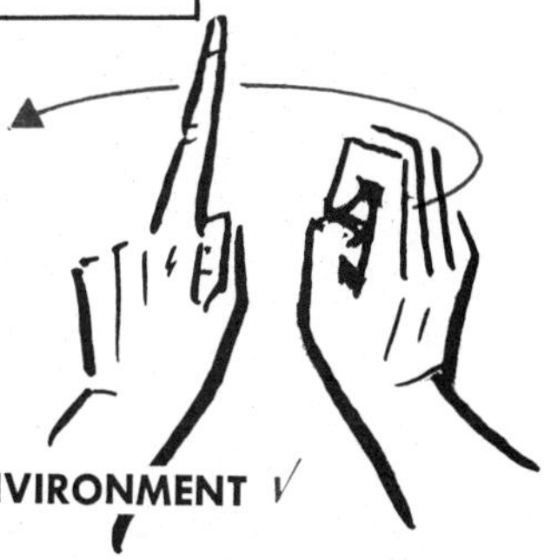

ENVIRONMENT

540

TROPIC √

TOOLS √

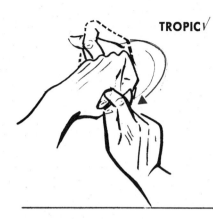

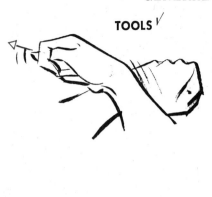

EQUATOR √

RESEARCH √

WELDING

HELIUM √

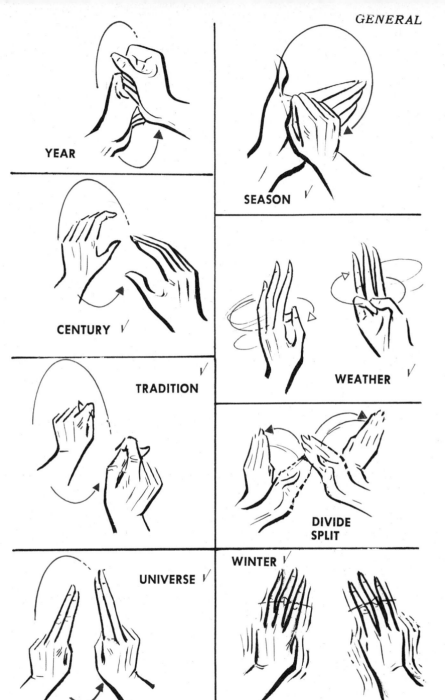

YEAR

SEASON ✓

CENTURY ✓

TRADITION ✓

WEATHER ✓

DIVIDE
SPLIT

UNIVERSE ✓

WINTER ✓

542

SOCIAL SECURITY "SS"

SOCIAL WORK (+ er) √

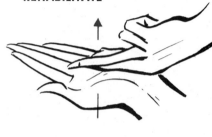

REHABILITATE √

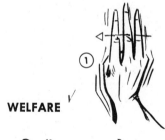

OPPORTUNITY √

WELFARE √

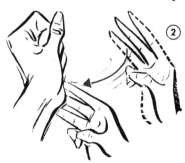

VOCATIONAL REHABILITATION

543

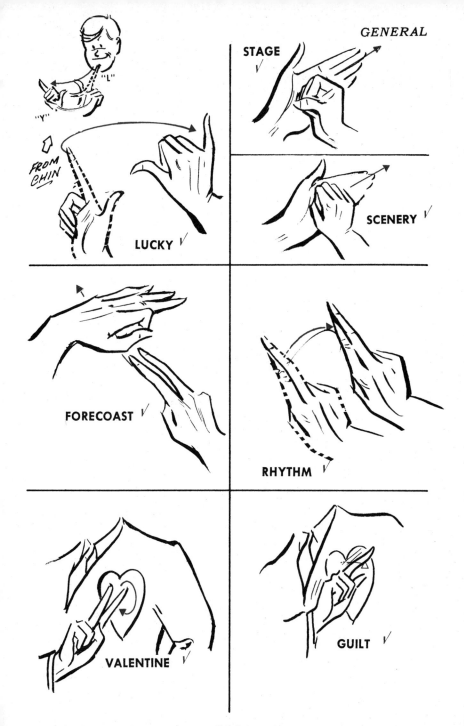

"L"

"Y"

FROM CHIN

LUCKY

STAGE

GENERAL

SCENERY

FORECOAST

RHYTHM

VALENTINE

GUILT

544

OBEY √

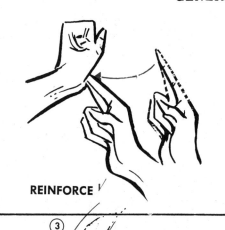

REINFORCE √

2 and 3 . . . √
ENGLAND

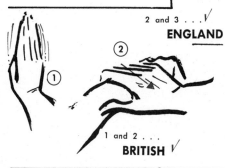

①

②

1 and 2 . . .
BRITISH √

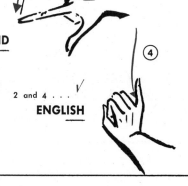

④

2 and 4 . . . √
ENGLISH

NOTE √

MEMO √

545

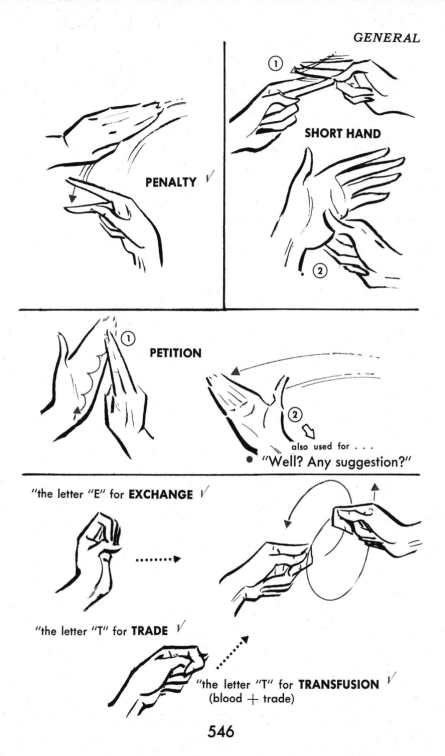

SHORT HAND

PENALTY

PETITION

also used for . . .

"Well? Any suggestion?"

"the letter "E" for **EXCHANGE**

"the letter "T" for **TRADE**

"the letter "T" for **TRANSFUSION**
(blood + trade)

546

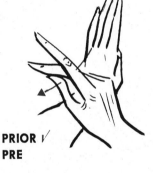

ORDER

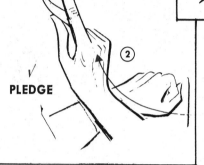

① ②

PLEDGE

PRIOR
PRE

PAMPHLET

move along edge of
hand

MAGAZINE

547

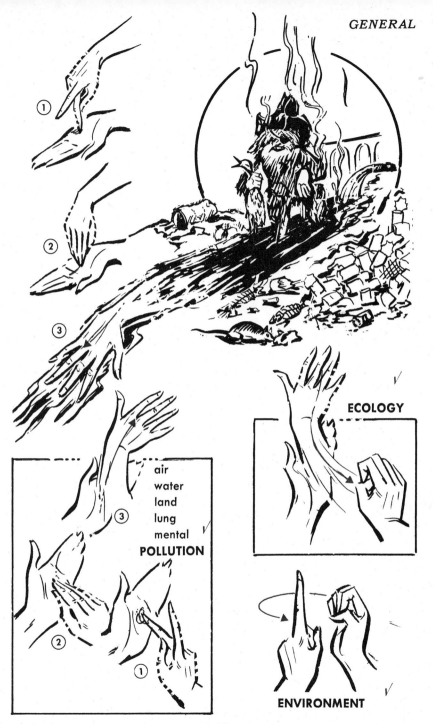

① ② ③

ECOLOGY

air
water
land
lung
mental
POLLUTION

③ ② ①

ENVIRONMENT

Index

• Denotes new signs developed in recent years

268.63
WAT Watson, David O.
Talk With Your Hands, Vol. 2

The Church of Christ
Tuscumbia, Alabama

The Church of Christ
Tuscumbia, Alabama